The Rhymers' Club

Poets of the Tragic Generation

The Rhymers' Club

Poets of the Tragic Generation

Norman Alford

MACMILLAN

First published 1994 by
MACMILLAN PRESS LTD
Houndmills, Basingstoke, Hampshire RG21 6XS
and London
Companies and representatives
throughout the world

ISBN 0–333–69440–6

A catalogue record for this book is available from the British Library.

10 9 8 7 6 5 4 3 2 1
06 05 04 03 02 01 00 99 98 97

Printed in the United States of America by
Haddon Craftsmen
Scranton, PA

PREFACE

IN the early 1890s, twelve poets and their guests met fairly regularly at Ye Olde Cheshire Cheese, the tavern off Fleet Street, and occasionally at other rendezvous. They called themselves the Rhymers' Club and included among their number W. B. Yeats, Arthur Symons, Ernest Dowson, Lionel Johnson, and John Davidson. Mention of this Rhymers' Club is made in Yeats's *Autobiographies* and there is a chapter on it in Dr. Mark Longaker's biography of Dowson. Eager to know more of its formation, its meetings, and general character, I pursued the subject further through memoirs and letters of which there are a great number concerning the period, and the result is this book.

In the course of my reading I came to see that, contrary to what I had been persuaded to believe, the poets of the 'nineties were not absorbed simply in deriving the maximum of sensation from life but were confronting the problem of the relationship which art could bear to life. The problem was as old as the Romantic movement itself, with its subjective emphasis. Tennyson had deserted 'The Palace of Art' for a 'cottage in the vale' where he might 'mourn and pray'; he had looked out of the Lady of Shalott's window and, unlike her, had survived the confrontation with life.

But some of the Rhymers: Yeats, Dowson, Symons—and other 'nineties writers who were not Rhymers—regarded Tennysonian optimism wrung from despair as an abdication rather than a triumph. They tried a return to the 'Palace of Art' which, it may be noted, Tennyson had left standing:

> '*Yet pull not down my palace towers, that are*
> *So lightly, beautifully built:*
> *Perchance I may return with others there*
> *When I have purged my guilt.*'[1]

Ernest Dowson—despite his adoption of Roman Catholicism—was not able to say, as did Tennyson:

> *I stretch lame hands of faith, and grope,*
> *And gather dust and chaff, and call*
> *To what I feel is Lord of all,*
> *And faintly trust the larger hope.*[2]

In his copy of Olive Schreiner's *The Story of an African Farm* he wrote:

> Faith, I think does pass, and Love, but Knowledge abideth. Let us seek Knowledge. At least let us shun emotion as we

would hell, for which it is a synonym. Let us live in ourselves and for ourselves. A reasonable self-love without passion or thought of others, and with end of self-culture before us, is better than a million emotions. Corollary—let us shun emotion and seek knowledge only . . . O.S. seems to admit that the ideal state is to be without hate, or love, or fear, or desire—passionless.[3] [These were injunctions which Dowson signally failed to heed in his own life, however.]

And, in spite of his love and admiration for Browning, Arthur Symons ignored the contempt revealed in 'Sordello' for the aesthete Troubador Eglamor:

He, no genius rare,
Transfiguring in fire or wave or air
At will, but a poor gnome that, cloistered up
In some rock-chamber, with his agate cup,
His topaz-rod, his seed-pearl, in these few
And their arrangement finds enough to do
For his best art . . .

Then, how he loved that art!
The calling marking him a man apart
From men—one not to care, take counsel for
Cold hearts, comfortless faces . . . since verse, the gift
Was his, and men, the whole of them, must shift
Without it . . .[4]

To Yeats, Dowson and Symons, among others, it seemed that Tennyson and Browning had evaded the problem of reconciling the pure vision of the creative self with the demands of a society whose culture offered instead of a temple, or a palace of art, a Crystal Palace stuffed with the grotesque ornaments of an industrialized, money-centred 'mass-cult.' The 'literature' of this society was a popular press which gave the newly literate groups of society a titillation of the senses and appetites instead of that knowledge of 'the best that has been thought and said' which had been Matthew Arnold's definition of culture.

The Rhymers were a brave few who came together for mutual support in the days when, as the cynical reviewer whom I quote on page 31 said: 'It is the malady of not marking that we are suffering from. Nobody can catch the public ear. The public does not care for twilights, and Love and Death; the public has an especial aversion to sonnets . . .'

As will appear, the Rhymers were not a school or a movement and widely differing conceptions of the connotations of 'Rhymers' Club' are to be found in criticism concerning the period. Yeats himself gives quite different emphasis in his article for the *Boston Pilot* (reproduced on p. 143), written in 1892, from that of his BBC broadcast in 1936. In 1892, Yeats wrote primarily of Arthur Symons, John Davidson, Richard Le Gallienne and, briefly, of fellow-Irishman John Todhunter. His remarks on Symons and Davidson which make up the body of the article stress the rejection of the Parnassian school of Gosse, Lang and Dobson with whom the ancient French form—form itself—was paramount. Yeats says of the Rhymers: 'they all believe that the deluge of triolets and rondeaus has passed away' (though Dowson, in fact, wrote rondeaus and villanelles of great charm) and that they were to 'set to music the deep soul of humanity.' They were not in quest merely of new forms but of new subject matter, new emotions, and thus Symons is the 'scholar of the music halls,' somewhat too distant—in Yeats's view—from his subject, while Davidson was at music halls also but there in mind and guts, too near to his subject, too full of fire and enthusiasm.

These observations of the young Yeats enable us to understand why a sensitive Dowson and Johnson were to be seen in the hearty (Samuel) Johnsonian environment of the Cheshire Cheese, with its ale and beefsteaks, which fellow-Rhymers Rolleston and Greene celebrated in verse of roistering mediocrity or downright doggerel. 'The cultivated man', Yeats wrote, 'has begun a somewhat hectic search for the common pleasures of common men and for the rough accidents of life.' And when Yeats describes the 'aesthete with a surfeit' and the 'Alastor tired of his woods and longing for beer and skittles' he is projecting on the other Rhymers very much of what was to become his own attitude, bending Symons towards that, and echoing the sentiments of John Davidson.

The account which Yeats gives in 1936 is quite different since he then remembers chiefly, as he admits, Dowson and Johnson. Through them he pictures the Rhymers as of the Decadence and thus contributes to the reputation which much criticism has given the Rhymers ever since. They sang, Yeats says, 'of wine and women' and it is evident that every Rhymer has now been subsumed in the image of Dowson who alone was the poet of that single theme.

REFERENCES

[1] Tennyson, 'The Palace of Art,' *The Poems and Plays of Lord Tennyson* (Oxford, 1963), p. 46.

[2] 'In Memoriam,' *ibid.*, p. 243.

[3] See Mark Longaker, *Ernest Dowson* (Philadelphia, 1945), p. 57.

[4] *The Poetical Works of Robert Browning* (London, 1929), I, 131.

I am most grateful to the authors, their executors and publishers for permission to quote from the following: *John Davidson, A Selection of His Poems,* edited by Maurice Lindsay (Hutchinson, Ltd), *The Letters of Ernest Dowson,* edited by Desmond Flower and Henry Maas (Cassell & Co., Ltd.), *Poems of Ernest Dowson,* edited by Mark Longaker (University of Pennsylvania Press, Philadelphia, 1962), A. Norman Jeffares, *W. B. Yeats, Man & Poet* (Routledge & Kegan Paul Ltd.), *The Complete Poems of Lionel Johnson,* edited by Ian Fletcher (Garnstone Press, Ltd.), Roger Lhombreaud, *Arthur Symons, A Critical Biography* (Garnstone Press, Ltd.), Mark Longaker, *Ernest Dowson* (University of Pennsylvania Press, Philadelphia, 1945); to Harvard University Press and the Fellows of Harvard University for permission to quote at length from *Letters to the New Island,* edited by Horace Reynolds; to Garnstone Press Ltd., and executors, for quotation from *Memoirs of a Misspent Youth* and *Author Hunting* by Grant Richards.

A similar debt of gratitude is due for permission to quote from Arthur Symons, *The Symbolist Movement in Literature,* edited by Richard Ellmann (E. P. Dutton & Co., Inc.),and I thank Professor Kathleen Tillotson for permission to quote from Geoffrey Tillotson, *Essays in Criticism & Research* (Cambridge University Press, 1942). I thank Michael Yeats and Macmillan London Limited for permission to quote from *The Collected Poems of W. B. Yeats,* W. B. Yeats's, *Essays & Introductions,* W. B. Yeats's *Autobiographies,* the *Bibliography of W. B. Yeats,* edited by Allan Wade, and Joseph Hone, *W. B. Yeats, 1865-1939* (Macmillan, 1962).

Norman Alford,
University of Victoria,
British Columbia.

CONTENTS

The Rhymers' Club

As once Rare Ben and Herrick
Set older Fleet-street mad,
With wit not esoteric,
And laughter that was lyric,
And roystering rhymes and glad:
As they, we drink defiance
To-night to all but Rhyme,
And most of all to Science,
And all such skins of lions
That hide the ass of time.
To-night, to rhyme as they did
Were well—ah! were it ours,
Who find the Muse degraded
And changed, I fear, and faded,
Her laurel crown and flowers.

CHAPTER I

The Beginnings of the Rhymers' Club

WHEN, in March 1888, John Butler Yeats moved his family for the second time into the Bedford Park 'garden suburb' of London, William Butler Yeats found the varieties of new–olde architecture less pleasing than they had seemed to him as a boy of twelve or thirteen. It was not that at twenty-three his pre-Raphaelite outlook had changed, for '. . . I was in all things pre-Raphaelite.'[1] But now he could view the attempt to realize pre-Raphaelite dreams in architecture with a more critical eye. Others had done so too and the region was no longer fashionable, thus suiting John B. Yeats's pocket which was seldom well-filled. The decline of the area and the criticisms which were voiced of the unpracticality of its buildings were symptomatic of the fading of pre-Raphaelitism under the hard light of a scientific realism which was more concerned with leaking roofs and bad drains than with the charm of the seventeenth-century panes of the Co-operative store. W. B. Yeats asserts that the roofs did *not* leak but the general opinion was a matter of sentiment rather than fact. John B. Yeats's painting which had pleased his poet son in its pre-Raphaelite heyday had already succumbed (the word which his son William would have used) to the influence of the realist school typified by Carolus Duran and Bastien-Lepage. None of his friends was now a pre-Raphaelite.

W. B. Yeats had met many of his father's friends in Ireland. At Bedford Park he met John Todhunter, York Powell, Florence Farr, Maud Gonne, Jack Nettleship, Edwin Ellis, and many others. Of these, Todhunter and Ellis were to become Rhymers' Club members and Nettleship a permanent guest. Todhunter was of Quaker stock. He had been educated at Trinity College, Dublin, and after studying at Vienna achieved some success in medicine. He held the Chair of English Literature at Alexandra College, Dublin for four years. He then migrated to London and devoted himself to writing poetry and plays. *The Sketch* (28 March, 1894) gave the following account of him at home: 'Dr. John Todhunter lives in that portion of Bedford Park which is called the Orchard, and his house bears the delightful name of Orchardcroft. Many of the Bedford Park houses are ideally pretty, but in too many of them one has to avert one's eyes from the window, whence one catches a dreary view of brickfields, to rest them on the pretty colouring and quaint effects within doors. Orchardcroft, however, in no aspect upon which it looks, does discredit to its country name. The almonds, which make a London March beautiful, are in full blow in Bedford Park, a drift of delicate purple-pink against the low house-fronts: seeing them, one realizes the great beauty of blossoms in detail without the crowding of leaves, a beauty to which, so far, the Eastern world has shown itself more sensitive than the West. Dr. Todhunter's study window, an oriel, long and low, looks over a succession of gardens, on the fruit-trees of which the hard buds that will presently break in rose and white are forming. When the leaves come in the garden of Orchardcroft and its neighbours that study window will look into boughs, and London seem far away. Dr. Todhunter in his study is well secluded from even the quiet thoroughfare of Bedford Park, and the terrible street-organ can only send him its jarring message muffled and indistinct.

'The study walls are in warm colours of dull red. The oriel, hung with blue draperies; the pot of white narcissus; the high wooden mantel; the fireplace with its old blue tiles: pictures and books and writing materials—the room had the indefinable look of refinement and high thinking which no planned-out effects can produce. Dr. Todhunter's handsome grey head, the head at once of the poet and the student, is well in place with the quiet surroundings. The one eccentric thing in the room was Mr. Aubrey Beardsley's strange poster announcing Dr. Todhunter's new play at the Avenue tomorrow: a lady, who is a mixture of Madame Chrysanthème and the daughter of Herodias as Mr. Beardsley imagined her, peering through a Japanese curtain of green discs on an indigo ground. What this great-shouldered, slanting-eyed person has to do with "A Comedy of Sighs" it is not easy to see.'

Edwin Ellis, poet and painter, had at one time shared a studio with John B. Yeats. According to Allan Wade, 'These two, with the painters J. T. Nettleship and George Wilson, sometimes called themselves "The Brotherhood".' Ellis lived for many years in Italy, where he farmed, and some unsigned paragraphs dealing with his life and the nature of his work, in which it is tempting to suspect the hand of Yeats, appeared in the *Bookman*, February

1893. The final paragraph reads, 'Mr. Ellis has now deserted Perugia, and is married and settled in London, pulling his old manuscripts from their corners, and shaking the dust from his old poems, and getting new ones written.'[2]

Bedford Park is in the far west of London, to the north of Chiswick High Road. About a quarter of an hour's walk along the latter, heading roughly westward, brought W. B. Yeats to the home of W. E. Henley. Yeats, in spite of an aversion to 'Henley's young men', mainly journalists, expressed in his letters at the time, described his contact with Henley (in his *Autobiographies*), as the beginning of his education. 'I disagreed with him about everything, but I admired him beyond words.'[3] Yeats disliked most of his realist poetry while Henley was affected by pre-Raphaelitism 'as some people are affected by a cat in the room.'[4] Some of the men whom Yeats met were Charles Whibley, Kenneth Grahame, Barry Pain, R. A. M. Stevenson, George Wyndham and Oscar Wilde.

At this stage of his career W. B. Yeats had published a few poems in the following Irish journals: *The Dublin University Review*, *The Irish Monthly*, *The Leisure Hour*, and *The Irish Fireside*[5] and, through John O'Leary's good offices was poet and correspondent for the two Irish-American papers, *The Providence Sunday Journal* and *The Boston Pilot*. His first book of verse (excepting the limited edition of *Mosada*, Dublin, 1886—100 copies) was published in January, 1889.[5] This was *The Wanderings of Oisin and Other Poems*, which he had completed late in 1887.[6] John O'Leary, the Fenian friend of the Yeats family, had worked up a subscription list sufficient to persuade Kegan Paul, Trench and Company to publish it. Thus the poet was launched in London to the tune of five hundred copies. He was also, through his meeting with Henley, introduced to the world of London periodicals; Henley took lyrics and essays (both of which he altered as he thought fit) for *The Scots Observer*.

Yeats declared himself a socialist for a time and in July, 1887, when his family was temporarily installed at Eardley Crescent, South Kensington, he had made his way to William Morris at Kelmscott House in Hammersmith. Here were held the Sunday evening debates of the Socialist League and Yeats had become one of the little group which stayed on to supper when the rest had gone. He met Walter Crane and several others concerned with the fine arts of book production and saw something of Bernard Shaw, Hyndman, and the anarchist Prince Kropotkin. But Yeats tired of socialism and of the attacks upon religion. Speaking up volubly at one of the meetings and ignoring the chairman's bell, he insisted that the change of heart needed for social reform could only arise from religion.[7]

Ernest Rhys, who is now best remembered as an editor for the Everyman series of books, first encountered Yeats at the Morris house and has recorded his impression of 'a tall, pale, exceedingly thin young man with a raven lock over his forehead.' They fell into conversation and eventually left the house together to wander eastward through the London streets. Yeats had missed his train but seemed to regard the appearance or non-appearance of trains as purely fortuitous and regaled Rhys with 'Irish gossip' until their parting at World's End Passage. A day or two later they met again and discussed the possibility of collecting Irish fairy tales for a Camelot series volume. Yeats had brought Crofton Croker's book of Irish tales. While they supped on cold bacon and cider, Yeats talked of Indian mysticism, Mohini Chatterjee, Madame Blavatsky and 'of Irish folk like Paddy Flynn, who had the secret of happiness, cooked mushrooms on a turf fire, and smiled in his sleep under a hedge.' Then there was another supper at the Yeatses', a lively house with two delightful girls and, over and above all, the father, 'a vehement Irishman, hot on politics.' Rhys's supper was somewhat spoiled by strong argument over Irish nationalism between father and son but in tranquil contrast he observed the mother, 'her strange dark eyes all but blind, who seemed nearest to her black-eyed son in mould.' In his upstairs room, the ceiling crudely painted by himself with signs of the Zodiac, Yeats showed Rhys his copy of Sir Samuel Ferguson's poems and also *Poems and Ballads of Young Ireland*, containing some of his own earliest poems. Rhys left with a verse of the 'Ballad of Father John O'Hart' ringing in his ears. Yeats's 'curious sing-song' had given it a strange and haunting resonance:

There was no human keening;
The birds from Knocknarea
And the world from Knocknashee
Came keening in that day.[8]

Yeats compiled *Fairy and Folk Tales of the Irish Peasantry*, as Rhys had suggested, working at it daily in the British Museum for about three months; it appeared in 1888 as number 32 of the Camelot shilling series. A little later, Putnam's commissioned his *Representative Irish Tales* (2 vols., 1891) which took longer. The tales were not all from old books; for Yeats included examples of his own fairyland verse and some of Douglas Hyde's translations from modern Gaelic stories.[9] The first book brought him about twelve pounds and the second twenty but he was happy in doing work which indirectly served his own purpose of bringing his nation's culture to a rebirth.

London oppressed him and he found vulgarity and materialism to be the English characteristics. He was most happy to escape each summer to his relatives in Sligo or to friends in Dublin. In London, he felt that he had already met most of the poets of his generation but that casual social contacts were not enough. He confided to Ernest Rhys: 'I am growing jealous of other poets and we will all grow jealous of each other unless we know each other and so feel a share in each other's triumph.'[10] Ernest Rhys was a poet of Welsh extraction who had produced some translations from the Welsh. He has recorded that Yeats's vision of Ireland made him consider whether he could bring about the rebirth of the culture which had produced the *Mabinogion.* He felt less able, being London-born, and half English by parentage.[11] Yeats and Rhys decided to try to begin a poets' club, to be called the Rhymers' Club, for the holding of regular meetings at the Cheshire Cheese, an old tavern which still flourishes in Wine Office Court, just off Fleet Street, and is where Doctor Johnson was at times happy to resort to 'that throne of all human felicity.'

In *Everyman Remembers*, Rhys says that T. W. Rolleston was the other of the Club's three founders.[12] Yeats brought in this friend of his father, who was one of O'Leary's most devoted disciples, a scholar in Greek, Gaelic, and German literature whom he had met often in Dublin at the Contemporary Club to which his father had taken him. He had met him also at Professor Edward Dowden's house in Dublin, along with the young Douglas Hyde and Stephen Gwynn. From August, 1885, Rolleston was editor of the *Dublin University Review.* In Dublin, Yeats had been commissioned to make the selection from the work of contemporary Irish poets already referred to, *Poems and Ballads of Young Ireland*, including three of his own poems and what is perhaps Rolleston's finest poem, 'Dead at Clanmacnoise,' the one that is most commonly anthologized.

Each of the three (Celtic) founders of the Rhymers' Club was to ask other poets to attend the projected club suppers and soon they reached the agreed total of ten. It may have been on Rhys's suggestion that Yeats called on Lionel Johnson at the 'Fitzroy settlement.' Herbert Horne, who did not actually join the club, being pre-eminently an architect and art scholar, but who visited from time to time, wrote to Rhys:

20 Fitzroy Street W.
9 Feb: 1890.

> . . . I asked the Rhymers here the other evening: Oscar came in at the end, after the rhymes were all over, and smiled like a Neronian Apollo upon us all. A kind of enthusiasm or inspiration followed. By the way, we at last obtained our faculty for Mrs. Gurney's chapel, last Saturday. So to celebrate the event I took dear Shields to eat at the Old C. Cheese. It was a new

> curiosity: the prophet Jeremiah in Fleet Street feasting upon Johnsonian steaks and ale—and delighted . . .![13]

Since Yeats and others refer several times to Horne it is as well to regard him as an unofficial Rhymer. Yeats had known him as early as March, 1888.[14] Rhys added the following note to this letter:

> Horne usually wrote with a reed pen which he cut himself. Mrs. Gurney's chapel was designed by Horne for her and the walls were frescoed by Frederick Shields, and the wall paintings have not lost by being toned down a little by London smoke and time, as the colours were almost too vivid. The chapel stands about a hundred yards west of the Marble Arch, facing the park, and on a hot day it is a pleasant retreat from the glare and noise of the busy highway.
>
> Before the Hobby-Horsemen moved to Fitzroy Street they had rooms in Southampton Street, Strand—No. 28—and here is an amusing note from Horne, inviting me to one of their Tuesday 'evenings':
>
> . . . We purpose also, with God's assistance, to open a most delightful-looking bottle (like an Urbino dish of Raphael's) filled with Chartreuse from the Certosa, yesterday arrived from Florence; also will be burnt Spikenard and Saffron; Calamus and Cinnamon; with all trees of Frankincense: Myrrh and Aloes; all the chief spices. If you do not turn up *now;* never again will I attempt to allure you into the immoral atmosphere of Southampton St.—no, not if I had all the arts of the Egyptians. . . .

Rhys continues:

> That is the missive of a sybarite; and in the end, I am afraid, he had to pay for his addiction to the fine savours and the epicurean cult. The sad thing was that his sybaritism, though masked by a spiritual aim, alienated him in the end from London colleagues like Selwyn Image and then from London itself. So, instead of keeping his collection of rare prints and art treasures to enrich his old home in Chelsea, he carried them off to Florence, which had already so many other art collections.

At the Fitzroy Street house in 1890 there lived, besides Horne, Lionel Johnson, Selwyn Image and Arthur Mackmurdo and, for a time, a friend of Johnson's named Arthur Galton. Yeats wrote that Image came constantly to the Rhymers' Club for a time, but he is not on the official list of members and permanent guests. He was a practising artist, illustrator, and designer of stained-glass windows who published a small volume of verse and later became Slade Professor at Oxford, the University of which he was a graduate.

Johnson had two spacious rooms near the top of the house and all of the residents shared a manservant.[15] In a music-room at the back Arnold Dolmetsch gave recitals of old music on the clavichord and other early instruments.

Horne and Mackmurdo edited *The Century Guild Hobby Horse* and Selwyn Image collaborated with them. Mackmurdo found the money for this lavish quarto magazine which is aptly described by Jepson as 'the link between the pre-Raphaelites and the poets of the 'nineties.'[16] 'It had a pre-Raphaelite cover, with a vignette of two Hobby-horsemen up to the neck in roses, along with flying birds and a shield with arrows sticking in it, that symbolled the aims of the group of Hobby-horsemen. . . . There was a preciosity about some of its pages, but it was a genuine attempt to give a new impetus to art and letters.'[17]

At 'Fitzroy', Yeats encountered the spirit of the movement against which his father had reacted and which he himself belonged to. Victor Plarr, who became a Rhymer, refers to a meeting at Fitzroy: 'The Rhymers held one memorable meeting in Mr. Herbert Horne's rooms in the Fitzroy settlement. They were then, so to speak, rediscovered and reconstituted, having previously been but a small group of Dublin poets.'[18] Plarr has ignored Rhys and is, perhaps, thinking of Rolleston, Todhunter and Yeats. Mr. Guy Harrison reproduces a list of members of the Rhymers' Club made by Dr. G. A. Greene, who was honorary secretary. The list is as follows:

John Davidson	(1857 – 1909)
Ernest Dowson	(1867 – 1900)
Edwin J. Ellis	(18 –)
George Arthur Greene	(1853 –)
Lionel Johnson	(1867 – 1902)
Arthur Cecil Hillier	(18 –)
Richard Le Gallienne	(1866 –)
Victor Plarr	(1863 –)
Ernest Radford	(1857 –)
Ernest Rhys	(1859 –)
Thomas Wm. Rolleston	(1857 –)
Arthur Symons	(1865 –)
John Todhunter	(1839 –)
Wm. Butler Yeats	(1865 –)

John Davidson, though a member of the club, did not contribute to the books. Besides members, the club had at one time affiliated to itself the following permanent guests: John Gray, Edward Rose, J. T. Nettleship, Morley Roberts, A. B. Chamberlain, Edward Garnett and William Theodore Peters. These names are from a list in the handwriting of Dr. G. A. Greene, who acted as honorary secretary to a club without rules or officers.

The list is from Guy Harrison's bibliography of Ernest Dowson, appended to Plarr (p. 131). I think that A. R. Chamberlain is intended. He was London correspondent of *The New York Sun*. John Gray (b. 1866) was an 'exquisite' young man who wrote poems and was a friend of Oscar Wilde; Wilde addressed him in some letters as 'Dorian' and paid for the publication of his *Silverpoints* (John Lane, 1893). Gray later became a priest. An interesting account of him appears in Rupert Croft-Cooke's *Feasting with Panthers* (London, 1967). Edward Rose (b. 1849) was a dramatist whose first London production, *Agatha Tylden*, was at the Haymarket Theatre in 1892. He was an actor for some years and drama critic for the *Sunday Times* from 1894 to 1896. He died in 1904. John Trivett Nettleship (b. 1841) was a painter, a friend of W. B. Yeats's father. He wrote *Robert Browning: Essays & Thoughts* (London, 1890) and, in 1898, a study of George Morland and his influence on some later painters.

Such a list as this has not, of course, quite the authority of a document contemporary with the group to which it relates. That it is not contemporary is, I think, sufficiently evidenced by the inclusion of terminal dates for those Rhymers who came to untimely ends. William Watson, whom Yeats describes as having joined, does not appear here. There were certainly several other fairly constant visitors such as Edgar Jepson.[19] Yeats wrote that sometimes, when the Rhymers met at a private house, Oscar Wilde came, as he did on the occasion already described. It would have been useless, Yeats wrote, to invite him to the Cheshire Cheese for he hated Bohemia.[20]

The Club did not reach the full membership strength shown in the list until about the middle months of 1891. Hence some commentators claim that the Club was formed in 1890 and others 1891.[21]

There were, of course, other clubs and rendezvous where some of the Rhymers were accustomed to meet for pleasure or serious purpose, from Yeats's Irish societies to The Odd Volumes and the Crown public house. As it is possible that the Rhymers borrowed certain customs from The Odd Volumes and as accounts of it are not, so far as I have been able to discover, very accessible, let us look in upon it before the serious business of Rhymers' Club meetings.

The Odd Volumes met on the first Friday of every month at Willis's Rooms in King Street, St. James's. 'The Sette of Odd Volumes to consist of twenty-one, this being the number of volumes of the Variorum Shakespeare of 1821: but supplemental O.V.'s to the number of twenty-one to be elected, and to be incorporated in the Sette as vacancies arise.'[22]

It is recorded, for the meeting of 3 October, 1890, that 'Mr. Edwin J. Ellis made a remarkable and interesting speech in relation to a rare work exhibited by the *Librarian*, namely, a coloured copy of Blake's "Jerusalem".' Ellis was the guest of Bernard Quaritch, who was to publish Yeats's and Ellis's study of Blake, and Arthur Symons was present as the guest of publisher John Lane, the Odd Volumes' secretary. On 7 November, 1890, Richard Le Gallienne, introduced by J. Roberts Brown, 'Alchemist,' was among guests including J. K. Jerome and John Tenniel.

Briefly, it was a place for a fine dinner, in good company, at which a talk on a curious subject would be given. 'Every new Odd Volume shall be expected, within a reasonable period of the date of his admission, to make a literary, scientific, or artistic contribution to the Sette.' In the words of the inaugural address: 'We do not look for learned and exhaustive treatises, nor for great artistic effects. Such are the work of the world and not its play.' On Thursday, 17 July, 1890, 'Brother' John Todhunter, Bard of the Sette of Odd Volumes, produced a dramatic sketch 'How Dreams Come True' at the Conversazione of the Sette at the Grosvenor Gallery. Florence Farr played Bertha, Hans Schwartz's daughter. Over 800 people had booked but only 375 arrived because of a storm.

Ernest Dowson was invited at least once:

> ... I had a charming evening at the Odd Vols last night. I sat opposite Todhunter who had three Irish guests (Rolleston, Percival Graves and Standish O'Grady, a charming Celt). My Lord Mayor came with a gorgeous creature to wait on him—Lane had three editors & Le Gallienne one. There was no one else there whom I knew—except by sight only—York Powell. . . .[23]

York Powell, a friend of the Yeats family, was a professor of history at Oxford.

The first explicit reference to the Rhymers in Dowson's letters is in a letter to Arthur Moore dated (by the editors) 2 February, 1891.[24] Dowson writes from the Grosvenor Club to which he had recently switched from the Arts & Letters:

> ... Thursday at Horne's was very entertaining: a most queer assembly of 'Rhymers'; and a quaint collection of rhymes. Crane (Walter) read a ballad: dull! one Ernest Radford, some triolets and rondels of merit: 'Dorian' Gray some very beautiful & obscure versicles in the latest manner of French Symbolism and the tedious Todhunter was tedious after his kind. Plarr and Johnson also read verses of great excellence; and the latter,

also, read for me my 'Amor Umbratilis'; And Oscar arrived late . . . in his voluminous dress clothes . . .'

Dowson met Arthur Symons for the first time in May 1891, and in June Dowson met Richard Le Gallienne for the first time.[25] Of Symons, Dowson wrote: 'on the whole, I was not greatly impressed'.

The Rhymers' Club was not conceived as a place for recreation in the broad sense of that word. Nor was it needed to supply a deficiency in social contacts, as we have seen. It was intended to achieve a greater degree of concentration on the craft of poetry, to be specifically a place for mutual audience and criticism.

REFERENCES

[1] W. B. Yeats, *Autobiographies* (London, 1961), pp. 113–115; Joseph Hone, *W. B. Yeats* (London, 1962), p. 57. These will be referred to hereafter as *Autobiographies* and Hone.

For an amusing account of Bedford Park see Ian Fletcher, 'Bedford Park: Aesthete's Elysium?' in *Romantic Mythologies*, ed. Ian Fletcher (London, 1967), p. 169.

[2] See *The Letters of W. B. Yeats*, ed. Wade (New York, 1955), p. 33 and p. 59.

[3] *Autobiographies*, p. 124.

[4] *Ibid.*, p. 125.

[5] Allan Wade, *A Bibliography of the Writings of W. B. Yeats* (London, 1951), pp. 285–288 and pp. 17–19.

[6] *The Letters of W. B. Yeats*, p. 54.

[7] *Autobiographies*, p. 148.

[8] Ernest Rhys, *Wales England Wed* (London, 1940), pp. 92–93.

[9] Hone, p. 59.

[10] *Autobiographies*, p. 164.

[11] *Wales England Wed*, p. 104.

[12] Ernest Rhys, *Everyman Remembers* (London, 1931), p. 105.

[13] Ernest Rhys, *Letters from Limbo* (London, 1936), p. 96.

[14] See *The Letters of W. B. Yeats*, p. 65.

[15] Hone, p. 78.

[16] Edgar Jepson, *Memories of a Victorian* (London, 1933).

[17] *Wales England Wed*, p. 109.

[18] Victor Plarr, *Ernest Dowson, 1888–1897: Reminiscences, Unpublished Letters, and Marginalia* (London, 1914), p. 63. Hereafter referred to as Plarr.

[19] See Edgar Jepson, *Memories of a Victorian*. Jepson was born in 1863 and was to write over sixty popular novels.

[20] *Autobiographies*, p. 165.

[21] See, for instance, Karl Beckson, 'New Dates for the Rhymers' Club', ELT XIII 1 (1970). See also Beckson's article on The Rhymers' Club in *Yeats Studies*, I (Dublin, 1971).

[22] *Odd Volume Year-Boke*. III (London, 1892. Priv. ptd.). For the year 1890–1891, *passim*.

[23] Extract from an undated letter reproduced in Dr. Mark Longaker's *Ernest Dowson* (University of Pennsylvania Press, 1945), p. 86, hereafter referred to as Longaker.

[24] *The Letters of Ernest Dowson*, ed. Desmond Flower and Henry Maas (London, 1967), p. 182. Dowson, who seldom dated his letters, has headed this one: 'Monday evening, In fest Pur: Virg', so there is virtually a supplied date. 'Dorian' Gray alluded to was John Gray, incorrectly supposed by many to be the original of Wilde's 'Dorian Gray'.

[25] *Ibid.*, pp. 200–201.

CHAPTER II

The Meetings of the Rhymers' Club

When I first went to London
I was looking for a technique;
I had the folk behind me
My good was there to seek:
But without the subtlety London taught
I could not learn to speak.

W. B. YEATS (recorded by Vernon Watkins).[1]

THE headquarters of the Rhymers' Club were 'in an upper room with a sanded floor'[2] at The Cheshire Cheese, off Fleet Street. The twelve members have been named (above, p. 7) as have also the 'permanent guests' and most of the fairly constant visitors. Selwyn Image and Herbert Horne maintained close connections with the Rhymers and Greene's not mentioning them may be due to the Rhymers having gone more often to them (at 'Fitzroy') than they to the Rhymers. Of the twelve members, Davidson did not contribute to either of the Club's anthologies, whose production will be described shortly, and A. C. Hillier contributed to the second one only. Francis Thompson came once to the Club and was asked to join but refused.[2]

The Rhymers would take supper with ale downstairs in the eighteenth-century coffee-house boxes and then adjourn to the upper room for their serious business. More ale, or punch, might be consumed and the poets smoked churchwarden pipes as they listened to one another's poems and criticized them.[3]

Jepson describes the room as gloomy and ill-lit, and the atmosphere as solemn. He first met Yeats there, 'wearing in those days the air of a Byronic hero, long-haired and gaunt, and delivering his poems in a harsh and high and chaunting voice.' Laughter was absent, smiles rare; the beards of Todhunter and Greene were forbidding, and all the poets were 'seething with the stern sense of their poetic mission.' Jepson describes Todhunter as 'aged' though he was, in fact, only in his fifties.[4] Several writers comment on the oddness of the association of gentle souls such as Johnson and Dowson with churchwarden pipes and bowls of punch. Yeats receives the palm as the best reader and Rhys's description of him reciting or intoning his verse 'with a musical voice and very haunting cadence'[5] balances Jepson's above: the two accounts are reconcilable, for the voice, as it comes to us from recordings, is at once harsh *and* musical, like the voices of many ballad-singers. Rolleston and Rhys would appear to have provided the robustness which found expression in the 'English and Johnsonian tradition' of these meetings (as Jepson puts it), and the former made up by his 'plain military style' for the others' want of vigour—the hushed voices of which Jepson complains, though he hushed his own in deference. Lionel Johnson's voice is described as demure and gentle and, by an unnamed visitor, as 'like a mouse's recitative.'[6] From a letter of Dowson's it appears that the Club was active in March, 1891:

> . . . I have just seen the proofs of my 'Cynara' poem, for the April *Hobby*. It looks less indecent in print, but I am still nervous! though I admire Horne's audacity. I read it, or rather Lionoel [*sic*] did for me, at the last Rhymers . . .[7]

Arthur Symons' account of the Club is disparaging. He, like Rhys, describes the pipes and ale but sees the meetings as feeble imitations of the exciting café groups with which he became very familiar in Paris. His attendance at meetings was sporadic but he is incorrect in surmising that Dowson also did not go very often.[8] Dowson's letters show that, before his affair with Adelaide Foltinowicz kept him away, he was a keen supporter of the Club. The following letter to Victor Plarr (written in October, 1892) may serve as an example of Dowson's interest:

> . . . I searched for you at the Independent Theatre the other night, but you were not. Meeting there, along with many other persons, the poet Green [*sic*], I undertook to send out notices for a Rhymers' meeting au Cheshire on Friday next . . . Will you take this in lieu of a post-card and endeavour to come. I have a quaint old German coming . . . whom you will appreciate . . .[9]

Richard Le Gallienne has described Dowson reciting his 'Cynara' poem at The Cheshire Cheese and romantically portrayed him as a painfully sensitive and delicate shadow of Shelley and Keats, worn and haggard 'with excessive ardours of too eager living.'[10] The 'Dowson legend', to which such a description as this was contributory, will be considered in a later chapter. We have seen that, according to Dowson, he asked Lionel Johnson to read his 'Cynara' poem for him. And Plarr wrote of Dowson that he refused ever to recite his poems at Rhymers' meetings, through shyness and a sense of his poorness as a reader.[11] Yet it will appear later that Dowson did, in fact, read his poetry upon occasion, probably when his mood had been enlivened by some drinks.

We have seen that the Rhymers' Club owed its inception to a simple desire among the poets to read and discuss their work with one another. Richard Le Gallienne indicates that the Club had no manifesto or propagandizing purpose and was an aggregation of individuals rather than a collective unit.[12] Thus any one meeting might be quite unlike another according to who was present. The approximate ages of some members in 1891 may be gathered from Dr. Greene's list.[13] Todhunter was fifty-two, Ellis forty-three, Greene thirty-eight, Rolleston and Radford thirty-four, Davidson also thirty-four, and Rhys thirty-two. The other members were all in their twenties. Dowson and Johnson were the youngest members. Le Gallienne points up the youthful appearance of Johnson in an anecdote concerning a Rhymers' Club evening at G. A. Greene's house. A small group of Rhymers were talking about poetry and Le Gallienne was surprised when they were spoken up to by a boy, seemingly of about fifteen, with an Oxford accent. The 'boy' continued to talk and display sufficient learning to silence the others. On enquiry he learned that this was Johnson, a twenty-three-year-old 'prodigy of learning'. He remarks that Johnson never seemed to look more than fifteen as long as he lived.[14]

W. B. Yeats describes the Club meetings as having been decorous and often dull. Their criticisms of one another seemed to take their polite tone from the 'hush-voiced' young Oxford men and were too polite to be of great value. Yeats found the oral testing of poetry to be a definition of their aims:

> *Love's Nocturne* is one of the most beautiful poems in the world, but no one can find out its beauty, so intricate its thought and metaphor, till he has read it over several times, or stopped several times to re-read a passage; and the *Faustine* of Swinburne, where much is powerful and musical, could not, were it read out, be understood with pleasure, however clearly it were read, because it has no more logical structure than a bag of shot.

I shall, however, remember all my life that evening when Lionel Johnson read or spoke aloud in his musical monotone, where meaning and cadence found the most precise elocution, his poem suggested 'By the Statue of King Charles at Charing Cross'. Nor will that poem be to me again what it was that first night.[15]

It may be useful here to collate the various comments on Johnson's reading voice, most of which have already appeared:

Commentator	Comment
Rhys:	'. . . demure, gentle voice . . .'
Rhys's 'visitor':	'. . . a mouse's recitative . . .'
Victor Plarr:	'. . . read marvellously as a man *periturus*.'
Yeats:	'. . . read or spoke aloud in his musical monotone, where meaning and cadence found the most precise elocution.'

Generally speaking, the Rhymers were anti-idealistic, opposed to generalization that could be explained or debated, and in this they were in reaction against the intrusion, as they saw it, into Victorian poetry of what Yeats called 'impurities'—curiosities about politics, about science, about history, about religion. Of these 'impurities' such great ones as Swinburne, Browning and Tennyson had been guilty. But Yeats himself, who attempted to understand what it was they opposed, found that he was just a single voice, and was regarded with suspicion for having 'ideas'. He told them at one time of his 'conviction that the world was now but a bundle of fragments' ('things fall apart, the centre cannot hold', as he wrote much later) and thereby plunged an already too silent evening into greater silence. Johnson would seem to have been a formidable silent antagonist: ' "Johnson", I was accustomed to say, "you are the only man I know whose silence has beak and claw".' It is ironical in retrospect that Yeats, who succeeded above all the others in founding a new tradition, should have felt somewhat ashamed of talking 'like a man of letters.' The 'young Irish poet, who wrote excellently but had the worst manners' and who described Yeats as talking thus, would appear to have been James Joyce. Unlike the others, Yeats was at this time obtaining his education—making up for his lack of a university education such as most of the others had. 'Lacking sufficient recognized precedent I must needs find out some reason for all I did.' He consequently felt himself a provincial, as were also Le Gallienne from Liverpool, Davidson from Greenock and Symons from Cornwall, but while their provincialism seemed curable, his own seemed incurable. Now, of course, we can be glad of this.

The opposition of the younger men, principally Johnson and Horne, to generalizations threatened to end all conversation whatsoever. Even Symons' venture, after a Paris visit, that 'We are concerned with nothing but impressions' brought silent sneers; for was not that too a generalization? 'Conversation constantly dwindled into "Do you like so and so's last book?" "No, I prefer the book before it".' Yeats attributes the Club's survival beyond the first difficult months to its Irish members (not including the only remotely Irish Johnson) who 'said whatever came into their heads.'[16]

In an undated letter to Plarr, presumably written about October, 1892, Dowson refers to Tennyson's death, and Dowson's comments on Victorian poets, though slight, complement Yeats's:

> ... Were you at the Rhymers last night? I wish I could have managed to be of the party. I suppose it is settled that we are to hold the Laurelship as a corporate office, and present the butt of Canary to the patron du Cheshire, as a composition for free drinks. I am sorry that Tennyson has crossed the bar: if only, that it leaves us so much at the mercy of Sir Edwin, L. Morris, Austen et Cie. But he was un grand poete, tout de même. Above all I love him because he did sacredly hate the mob—which whether it be the well-dressed mob whom Browning pandered to, or the evil-smelling mob to which William Morris does now to the detriment of his art and the offence of his own dignity still pander, I hold alike to be damnable, unwholesome and obscene.[17]

It may be noticed that, in expressing disgust at 'the evil-smelling mob,' Dowson is being more widely condemnatory than a Wilde or a Verlaine whose desire to shock was confined to the bourgeois.

However, it would probably be wrong to take Dowson's remarks here too seriously—his point is that the writer should not be swayed by any kind of regard for a crowd.

The account which Yeats gives of the Rhymers' sartorial habits might suggest that they did not attempt *épater le bourgeois* by dress. He would have us believe that his own brown velveteen coat, loose tie, and very old Inverness cape were not deliberately chosen for their poetical appearance but were accidental accretions. Most of the Rhymers, he tells us, would not have shown themselves in any costume other than 'that of an English gentleman.' Exceptions were Le Gallienne, who wore a loose tie, and Symons, whose Inverness cape was 'quite new and almost fashionable.' Lionel Johnson's theory was that one should be quite unnoticeable. Apparently this restraint was to some extent compensated for by extreme individualism in handwriting.[18]

For deliberate opposition to Yeats one could hardly do better than cite George Moore, even in this, admittedly trivial, instance. When Moore saw the young Yeats he was

> . . . striding to and forth at the back of the dress circle, a long black cloak drooping from his shoulders, a soft black sombrero on his head, a voluminous black silk tie flowing from his collar, loose black trousers dragging untidily over his long, heavy feet. . . .[19]

However this may have been, it seems unlikely to me that Yeats was consciously 'on exhibition' as Moore charges. A different case was Le Gallienne. Rhys noted something histrionic in his make-up and commented on the glossy black hair, cloak and slouch hat with which he courageously faced the prosaic London world.[20] Generally, it seems that the aim of most of the Rhymers was to dress as well as possible and, remembering the different fashions of those days when a man's class and kind of occupation were revealed by dress, we may infer that they dressed as 'gentlemen' at a time when dandyism was not limited (as indeed it is not at the present time) to practitioners of the arts.

The Rhymers' Club consisted of men of high hopes but no assurance of success. The fact that some of their work had appeared in periodicals and that a few small volumes of verse had appeared (mainly by private subscription) was no guarantee of their potential fame, especially when the editors of these periodicals, as was not infrequently the case, were friends or even intimates of the poets. Yeats relates:

> I had now met all those who were to make the 'nineties of the last century tragic in the history of literature, but as yet we were all seemingly equal, whether in talent or in luck, and scarce even personalities to one another. I remember saying one night at the Cheshire Cheese, when more poets than usual had come, 'None of us can say who will succeed, or even who has or has not talent. The only thing certain about us is that we are too many.'[21]

To some it seemed that Dowson was the most promising Rhymer. Rhys wrote:

> At that time the one Rhymer we believed to be most potential in the group was Ernest Dowson. Not that he was able to make the rhythm tell, when he read his poems; but they had an individual savour unlike that of any other poet, which seemed to point to the rarer imaginative work he might yet do.[22]

There were two rather special events in the life of the Club in 1891: one was a send-off supper for Ernest Rhys on the eve of his wedding[23] and the other a special meeting for the lady whom Yeats was to desire but to be unable to marry:

> . . . We had a 'Rhymers' meeting at Ellis's for Miss Gonne who has now departed for Paris where she stays for a week, or ten days more probably, and then returns here for a few days and so back to Dublin.[24]

Some account of Rhymers' Club meetings is given by Don Patricio Gannon in the introduction to his slim selection of Rhymers' Club poets. Unfortunately, the source of his information is not given. He claims that the reading of poems was always done in alphabetical order and that at one time Victor Plarr proposed a fine of sixpence for anyone using the word 'lily', singular or plural.[25] Certainly this flower was wilting from over-use in their verse as in that of a number of their contemporaries.

Several members began, after a while, to be dissatisfied with the desultory nature of some of the meetings. It is not surprising, in the light of what has been said earlier, that Yeats was one of these who sought some kind of set programme. Victor Plarr describes how he and Dowson and Yeats stayed on at a meeting in Johnson's rooms after the rest had gone:

> Mr. Yeats proposed that we should in future debate on poetry, and by way of beginning he made a speech, pointing out that poetry had at one time passed through four stages, which were, I think, the Diabolic, the Seraphic, the Celestial, and something else. In the interests of truth it fell to my ungrateful lot to point out that poetry originated among savages and consisted at first of not much more than lists of laudatory titles, chanted again and again by hunters or warriors in praise of the successful men among their number. Ernest Dowson scented modern science here, became uneasy, and voted down poetry debates in future.
>
> From one point of view he was right, for, at the present moment, 'chatter about Shelley', and poetry debate generally, account for much of our sterility, timidity and lack of enthusiasm.[26]

The detestation of 'modern science' was common to most of the Rhymers, not least Yeats himself, of course. To them as to Blake the sun was something more than a flaming ball of gas. Yeats attributes his failure to become intimate with Horne then to his suspicion that he and his painter and architect friends had become lukewarm in their pre-Raphaelite faith. Horne's church, in the manner of Inigo Jones, mentioned earlier, displeased Yeats then, although he later came to consider it a little masterpiece, because it was in his view representative of that eighteenth century which in the young Yeats's opinion:

. . . taught a school
Of dolts to smooth, inlay, and clip, and fit
Till, like the certain wands of Jacob's wit,
Their verses tallied.[27]

Yeats's efforts to formalize the Rhymers' Club meetings were not such, as we have seen, to appeal to Dowson and Johnson. The proposals of G. A. Greene smacked even more of the organized literary society and yet some attempt was made to implement them. He compiled a list of the anniversaries of the great English poets in preparation for a series of Anniversary Nights at the Club. Among those to be commemorated were Pope, Shenstone and Marlowe. Each Rhymer was to bring a poetic tribute to the bard of the night. On the Marlowe night, Ernest Rhys was without his rhyme and was ordered to invent one on the spot. After a while, and in a retaliatory vein, he recited:

ON MARLOWE

With wine and blood and reckless harlotry,
He sped the heroic flame of English verse;
Bethink ye, Rhymers, what your claim may be,
Who in smug suburbs put the Muse to nurse?[28]

In fact, only some of the Rhymers lived in the smug suburbs. Perhaps these had been the most clamorous for his rhyme.

Rhys gave an account of this particular evening in a letter, dated 9 July, 1890, to the American critic and poet, Edmund Clarence Stedman:

> You ask about our 'Rhymester's Club.' We had a very jolly meeting last Friday,—a sort of Marlowe night, as that afternoon a benefit performance for the Marlowe Memorial had been given at the 'Shaftesbury'. John Davidson—author of 'Scaramouch in Naxos' & ot[her] most original plays, lately much discussed; Willie Yeats, a young Irish poet; T. W. Rolleston, another Irish poet, or rhymester, to use the Club term; Nettleship, the painter, O'Leary, the old Irish rebel; & two or three others less notable were there. Not a large gathering, you see; but a right jovial & friendly one.

Rhys goes on to describe how, because he had not his rhyme ready, he was 'exiled to a far corner with a glass of crystal fluid at his elbow, & bidden compose a quatrain there & then, or—die!'

When he had read his satirical lines, there was an uproarious scene and Rhys, 'feeling his life in danger, escaped incontinently into the rain without, & so home!' Rhys describes the place of meeting, the 'Old Cheshire Cheese' to Stedman and mentions that the American, Henry Harland (later to edit the *Yellow Book*), had attended a previous meeting.

In general, however, meetings seem to have been quiet and even dull. Such was that of which C. Lewis Hind gives an account in *Napthali*. It was held in the drawing-room of Todhunter's home. Hind says that Todhunter

> was a kind of sedate father of the Rhymers' Club, and that meeting in his house, at any rate, was dull and decorous. Most of the poets talked most of the time with articulated precision about quantitative equivalents, and, with the exception of courteous Dr. Todhunter, no one seemed to notice the guest of the evening—Francis Thompson. We—that is, Vernon Blackburn and I—had brought him there by special request. I wish the meeting had been held at that 'pub between two stage-doors'. Bedford Park seemed to awe those tame young poets. Francis Thompson sat next to Ernest Dowson, but I did not see them speak to one another. The 'Nineties poets were often like that —remote, shy, aloof.[29]

There was not, perhaps, much relation between this versifying for social entertainment of the Marlowe night and the more serious thought and work of the Rhymers. But even Apollo, as Horace wrote, did not always keep his bow bent, and this was probably the nearest the Rhymers came to unbending. Of course, the social function *was* important to men who believed in a poetry which was to be heard, whether spoken or sung. Yeats refers to this and remarks upon some of Dowson's poems:

> They were not speech but perfect song, though song for the speaking voice. It was perhaps our delight in poetry that was, before all else, speech or song, and could hold the attention of a fitting audience like a good play or good conversation, that made Francis Thompson, whom we admired so much—before the publication of his first poem I had brought to the Cheshire Cheese the proof sheets of his *Ode to the Setting Sun*, his first published poem—come but once and refuse to contribute to our book. Pre-occupied with his elaborate verse, he may have seen only that which we renounced, and thought what seemed to us simplicity, mere emptiness.[30]

Yeats refers to this encounter with Francis Thompson again in his introduction to *The Oxford Book of Modern Verse* (p. x):

> I read out at a meeting of the Rhymers' Club a letter describing Meynell's discovery of Francis Thompson, at that time

still bedded under his railway arch, then his still unpublished *Ode to the Setting Sun.*

On 23 April, 1892, Yeats wrote a description of the Club for the *Boston Pilot*, which I have reproduced on pages 143–144.

REFERENCES

[1] Quoted by A. N. Jeffares in his *W. B. Yeats, Man and Poet* (London, 1949), p. 48.

[2] Yeats, *Autobiographies*, p. 165.

[3] Rhys, *Everyman Remembers*, p. 105.

[4] Jepson, *Memories of a Victorian*, p. 235.

[5] *Op. cit.*, p. 103.

[6] *Everyman Remembers*, p. 105.

[7] Longaker, p. 81. The letter is dated by Longaker. It is addressed to Sam Smith, an Oxford friend of Dowson's.

[8] Arthur Symons' preface to his edn. of Dowson's *Poems* (London, 1905), p. x.

[9] Longaker, p. 103.

[10] Richard le Gallienne, *The Romantic '90s* (London, 1925), p. 186. Hereafter referred to as Le Gallienne.

[11] Plarr, p. 66.

[12] Le Gallienne, p. 184.

[13] See above, p. 7.

[14] Le Gallienne, p. 188.

[15] Yeats, *Autobiographies*, p. 301.

[16] Yeats, *Autobiographies*, pp. 165–166, 189.

[17] Plarr, p. 62,

[18] *Autobiographies*, p. 167.

[19] George Moore, *Ave* (London, 1911), p. 45.

[20] Rhys, *Everyman Remembers*, p. 114.

[21] *Autobiographies*, p. 170.

[22] Rhys, *Everyman Remembers*, p. 103.

[23] Rhys, *Letters from Limbo*, p. 90.

[24] *The Letters of W. B. Yeats*, ed. Wade (New York, 1955), p. 67. The letter referred to, dated November, 1891, is to John O'Leary.

[25] Patricio Gannon, *Poets of the Rhymers' Club* (Buenos Aires, 1953).

[26] Plarr, p. 63.

[27] See *Autobiographies*, pp. 168–169.

[28] The incident is recorded in a footnote to the poem in *The Book of the Rhymers' Club* (London, 1892).

[29] For the reference to *Napthali* (New York, 1926) and particulars of Rhys's letter to E. C. Stedman I am indebted to James G. Nelson, *The Early Nineties: A View From the Bodley Head* (Harvard University Press, 1971). The Rhys letter is in Columbia University Library.

[30] *Autobiographies*, p. 301.

CHAPTER III

The Books of the Rhymers' Club

THE most successful proposal aimed at providing some kind of direction to the activities of the Rhymers' Club was for the compilation of an anthology. Yeats says it was his proposal and that he made it because he was anxious to have copies of the poems of Dowson which he knew only from Dowson's reading of them.[1] (Incidentally, this is part of the evidence that Dowson did read his poems.) Yeats wrote to Elkin Mathews on 12 November, 1891, to arrange to visit him in company with Johnson and Greene in order to discuss the project. By the 23rd, Mathews had agreed to support it.

It may be coincidence that in a letter to Ernest Rhys dated 20 October, 1891, Edmund Gosse had also suggested some kind of anthology. His letter illustrates the general difficulty of publishing poetry then, and I shall therefore quote most of it:

> My Dear Mr. Rhys,
>
> I was very glad indeed to see your writing, though I should have been more glad to see your face. You give me a brave and cheerful account of your life, but I am afraid it involves a good deal that needs cheerfulness and courage to sustain.
>
> Thank you for letting me read your very beautiful lyric 'A London Rose'. I have not seen anything of yours which I have liked better, if so much. I wish I could suggest anything sensible about the publishing of your book. It seems more difficult than ever to sell verse. I have been trying to find a publisher for Arthur Symons, alas! without success. It seems to me that it would be rather a good plan if four or five of the very best of you young poets would club together to produce a volume, a new

Parnassus, and so give the reading public a chance of making your acquaintance. . . .[2]

The Rhymers began to plan their volume. Dowson was enthusiastic and energetic in furthering the practical arrangements. He wrote to his fellow-Rhymer, Plarr, who had been absent through sickness, to explain the suggested procedure:

Bridge Dock

Mon Cher Victor

I am grieved at this long absence of yours, but I hope it implies nothing worse than convalescence, and that we shall soon have you once more with us. In the mean time, I write to you, as an official exponent of the sentiments of the 'Rhymers' at their last meeting, and at their request, to ask, if we can count on you, as a contributor to 'The Book of the Rhymers' Club' which it is proposed to issue, in an inexpensive manner in the autumn. The Rhymers, to be represented in it are, pretty much as follows:

Yeats
Greene
Johnson
Dowson
Radford
Le Gallienne
Ellis
*Ghose
*Symons
*Rolleston
Todhunter
*Rhys

NB. Those names with asterisks attached, are those of persons, who have not yet *definitely* promised to join in the scheme. May we add your name definitely to these? The expense will be *very small*, as it will be distributed amongst all in proportion to the pages given to each; and in view of their number, and the fact that the maximum of space allowed to any Rhymer is 6 pieces: it could not very well be any thing than inconsiderable; profits of course, if any, on the same scale. We count on your consent. Assuming it then, as given, I have to inform you that at the last meeting it was arranged, as to order of sending in & selecting rhymes, that Johnson should be, as a central person, intending to be in town, all the summer, appointed a sort of receiver of all the verses, although the selection is either to be made by the whole Club in council (wh. seems to me impracticable) or by a committee of 3 to be subsequently selected: 2nd that the maximum of pieces is to be 6 & the minimum 3 (probably). 3rd that each rhymer is exhorted to send in *double* the number of pieces he wishes inserted—say 12 for 6, 10 for 5 etc & that he may mark them in the preferential order he gives to them himself: & must state, where & when, if at all, they have been published. 4th. that the verses should be sent if possible to Johnson before the 26th inst: in order that they may be put before the House at the next meeting of the Rhymers & the book be got under way *quam celerrime*.

I have now, I think discharged my duty, in I hope a fashion not too obscure to be intelligible. We pray you to give your adherence to this notion & send your rhymes forthwith: or better still recover your health & come back to the Cheshire Cheese before the 26th: this is our prayer. But I see the post goeth: please remember me very kindly to your people.

Yrs ever

ERNEST DOWSON[3]

From another letter of Dowson's to Plarr, written some time in March, 1892, soon after the *Book of the Rhymers' Club* had appeared, we learn that 'the edition is entirely exhausted.' Dowson's keen interest in the reception of the book appears:

> ... Thanks muchly for your cuttings and the letter which is most charming and polyglot! I return you all herewith save the *Daily Chronicle*, which I should like to keep as you have another, and the *Daily News*, which I will send you tomorrow, when I have shown it to my people. I am amused to find that my cursory acquaintance with the Anthology of Anthologies has made such a deep impression on my manner—or can it be that my reviewer does not know what the Gr. Anthology is about? I didn't go to the Rhymers last night, nor to the last meeting but one; chiefly because the meetings were in inaccessible places and the night was cold, and partly because I was in a condition too lyrical even for the society of poets. So I have not run across Green; but you will be glad to hear that the edition is entirely exhausted. I have seen scarcely anyone lately but Gray and Hall; once for a short time Horne, & for a moment, Image: and there have been accidental meetings. In effect I am become far too absorbed to do anything but sit, in Poland, and gather the exquisite moments....

As a postscript Dowson wrote: 'Dear Image! How charming his notice is. I had already obtained it.'[4]

450 copies of the *Book of the Rhymers' Club* were printed. Of these, 350 were issued for sale. Elkin Mathews was the publisher, not John Lane, as is often stated. Lane and Mathews collaborated

a little later. 'Poland' was the name given by Rhymers and friends to a restaurant at 19, Sherwood Street, Soho, kept by a Polish couple. Dowson became infatuated with their daughter, Adelaide Foltinowicz, who was about thirteen years old at this time.

Concerning Elkin Mathews, Professor James G. Nelson writes (*op. cit.*, p. 22):

> It is doubtful that any other publisher was approached by the club. By the fall of 1891, the Bodley Head already had established itself as the publishing house of choice so far as the younger and more promising of the poets were concerned. Moreover, Le Gallienne, Ernest Radford, John Todhunter, and Walter Crane were among the Rhymers who were by this time Bodley Head authors. Then, too, Mathews must have been fairly well known to the group since he lived in Bedford Park next door to the Yeats family and not far from the Todhunters' residence. It is also very possible that Mathews had been something of a permanent guest of the club for some time. In a letter to the publisher dated 13 January, 1891, Ernest Radford, requesting Mathews to forward to Cosmo Monkhouse an invitation to a Rhymers' Club meeting, went on to issue one to Mathews himself. 'I believe,' he wrote in a postscript, 'you do not rhyme but I shall be very glad if you will join us.'

For convenience of reference I have appended on pages 147–149 a resumé of the contents of the Books of the Rhymers' Club. The *Daily Chronicle* review, to which Dowson refers, appeared on 26 February, 1892, and I will here reproduce it in full:

A ROUND TABLE OF RHYMERS

'*Sweet are the pleasures that to verse belong,*
And doubly sweet a brotherhood in song.'

wrote the youthful Keats to George Felton Mathew.

A volume by twelve young rhymers is promising food for the middle-aged cynic. It was evidently too great a temptation for Mr. Lang the other day. All seems fish that comes to Mr. Lang's net—a serious charge against an angler. 'The *Quarterly*, savage and tarterly' has the reputation of killing a certain poetical cock-robin. Mr. Lang is more ambitious and would try his bow and arrow on a round-robin. Ah, but that's a very different matter! A poet with twelve heads, as this Rhymers' Club may be described, is a hydra which needs some killing. Besides, the cynic must be very determined who could find many chinks for his arrows in *The Book of the Rhymers' Club*, which twelve Fleet-street nightingales have sung together with their breasts against a quill.

These rhymers are evidently wise youths. They have put on the armour of common sense. They have come with no airs of genius—no red-hot artistic propaganda. They have followed that great precept of 'the seven sages', and known themselves. They have outlived the illusions of new 'movements' and 'schools', having well digested their Ecclesiastes. 'Is there anything whereof it may be said, See, this is new? It has been already of old time, which was before us.' Therefore they write calmly, as though—ahem!—'not for an age, but for all time.' They are in no hurry to be heard; they are not over-confident that they are worth hearing. But still they write rhyme, for the same reason that the late Mr. Matthew Arnold drank wine, because they like it.

Though surprised and delighted to find such common sense in 'heavenly minds', one rather fears it as an omen for the poetical future of the gentlemen concerned. A little more of the furore of promise, a little less of the calmness of maturity might have encouraged the spirit of prophecy within us.

> *Set fools upon their folly!* [*sic; upon* should be *unto*]
> *Our folly is pure wit,*
> *As t'were the Muse turned jolly;*
> *For poets' melancholy—*
> *We will not think of it,*

sings Mr. Ernest Rhys in a neat prologue. But then 'folly' is just the quality absent from this book; the divine 'folly' of an impulse that through joy and anguish pours out a fiery heart in song. But these rhymers, they—'will not think of it'. They are too much at home in the world; too grateful for the benefits of civilization, in the shape of comforts both 'solid' and liquid. They belong to too good clubs. They have not a particle of 'Alastor' in their compositions, and if their 'songs must tears beget', it must certainly be by someone else's tears, and not according to Rossetti's prescription. It is true that in an epilogue Mr. E. A. Greene [*sic*] sings:

> *Ours be the task to prolong*
> *The joy and the sorrow of song,*
> *In the mist of years that begrime;*
> *In the clinging mist of the years,*
> *With reverent toil and with tears,*
> *To hammer the golden rhyme,*
> *Hammer the ringing rhyme*
> *Till the mad world hears.*

Mr. Greene would seem to be accredited, by italics,[5] as spokesman of the club, but, we would ask, is there not here an uncharacteristic strain of 'youthful' earnestness?

The Rhymers' Club

To 'Hammer the ringing rhyme Till the mad world hears'? Nonsense. We don't believe it of them. The rhymers have no such intention we are sure. They don't care anything about 'the mad world'. We don't think they believe in its madness either. They are far too agreeable—and selfish. All they want is to be left alone at 'The Cheshire Cheese', and—

As once Rare Ben and Herrick
Set older Fleet-street mad,
With wit not esoteric,
And laughter that was lyric,
And roystering rhymes and glad:
As they, we drink defiance
To-night to all but Rhyme,
And most of all to Science,
And all such skins of lions
That hide the ass of time.
To-night, to rhyme as they did
Were well—ah! were it ours,
Who find the Muse degraded,
And changed, I fear, and faded,
Her laurel crown and flowers.

However, both the club spokesmen are somewhat harder on their community than they need be. For though we cannot profess to descry a Big 'Ben', or exactly a Herrick, in their book, it is by no means a mediocre performance. The Rhymers' Club do not *hammer* their rhyme, nor is their muse as degraded, changed, and faded as Mr. Rhys pretends. Mr. Rhys himself contributes a really fine ballad in the old English manner, a form much overworked, but seldom filled with such genuine impulse as in 'The Wedding of Pale Bronwen':

Beneath the sea pale Bronwen lies,
Red Ithel beneath the sand;
But they are one in Holy Church,
One in love's Holy Land.

Red Ithel lies by Jerusalem town,
And she in the deep sea lies;
But I trow their little babe was born
In the gardens of Paradise.

And though the volume, like all young verse, bears marks of influence, several of its contributors possess distinct, if not very violent individualities. The roll-call of the Club is as follows: Messrs. Ernest Dowson, Edwin J. Ellis, E. A. Greene [*sic*], Lionel Johnson, Richard Le Gallienne, Victor Plare [*sic*], Ernest Radford, Ernest

Rhys, T. W. Rolleston, Arthur Symons, John Todhunter, W. B. Yeats. Of these Messrs. Johnson, Le Gallienne, Radford, Symons, and Yeats stand out foremost. Mr. Dowson, too, has a very sweet gift, though a little consumptive, and perhaps fed too much on the Greek Anthology. Of Messrs. Rhys and Greene we have already spoken. Mr. Rolleston has a gallant ballade of the 'Cheshire Cheese', in which he truly remarks that, whatever else may fail us,

No phantoms are the ale
And beefsteaks of the Cheshire Cheese.

Of the five other gentlemen selected four have already won a leaf or two of laurel, and Mr. Yeats, Mr. Le Gallienne, and Mr. Symons are all shortly to be seen at full length in new volumes. Perhaps it will be better for us to wait till those volumes appear before quoting them, seeing that we near the end of a column. But this we will say: that if they intend giving us more poems such as those which represent them here, we shall have to begin to take them seriously. Mr. Lionel Johnson had better join them and bring out his volume, too; for his poems are quite among the best in the book. We know well of him as a critic. He, it will be remembered, is to write a study of Thomas Hardy. Mr. Johnson's individuality is piquant as being somewhat out of fashion—that of a Royalist and a Catholic. His best poem is, perhaps, that on 'The Statue of King Charles the First at Charing Cross' . . . [Here the poem is quoted in full.] . . . We like 'Plato in London' next best; but 'The Last Music' is very full of solemn sweetness:

Surely she hath lain so an hundred years:
Peace is upon her, old as the world's heart.
Breathe gently, music! Music done, depart:
And leave me in her presence to my tears,
With music in mine ears;
For sorrow hath its art.

Mr. Robert Bridges' 'Elegy' is richer, and of a fuller music; but Mr. Johnson's requiem is none the less a beautiful poem.

Altogether the Rhymers have no reason to be ashamed of their 'Book'. They can afford to let the distinguished middle-aged critic sneer. The company at the Mermaid would have accepted the little book in a different spirit. Can't you see how Herrick would have turned once more to remind his 'Saint Ben' of *their* old

. . . lyric feasts
Made at the Sun,
The Dog, the Triple Tun.

Concerning Andrew Lang's reviewing, W. B. Yeats wrote to his father (21 July, 1906): '. . . Andrew Lang was hardly civil when I sent him my first book, and very uncivil indeed when he reviewed the Rhymers' book. Two years later he wrote a very generous article of apology. He excused himself by saying that new work was very difficult to him, and that when he first read Verlaine's poetry he thought it no better than one finds in the poet's corner of a country newspaper.'[6]

Richard Le Gallienne notes, in retrospect, that the *Book of the Rhymers' Club* was simply a miscellany such as *England's Helicon* or Davidson's *Poetical Rhapsody* had been. It brought together 'in friendly association', the work of twelve mostly young poets, recently arrived in London. We have seen that Le Gallienne disclaimed any propagandizing purpose on the part of the Club; he goes on to deny revolutionary aims and says that, as a body, the Club was neither energetic nor long-lived. There was no central artistic ideal common to all its members as there was in, say, the subsequent Imagist movement. 'Each was doing his own work in his own way.' Some of the Rhymers were to become 'representatives of their period, initiators of certain of its poetic trends,' and the *Book of the Rhymers' Club* contained poems which have since found places in better known and larger anthologies.

Encouraged by the successful sales of their first book, and relishing the stimulus of publication, the Rhymers set to work to compile the *Second Book of the Rhymers' Club*, which appeared in 1894. Five hundred copies were printed for Britain, of which only 400 were for sale. There were, however, another 50 copies in a large paper edition. One hundred and fifty copies were printed for America where the distributors were Dodd, Mead and Company of New York.

'The numbers mentioned do not include the copies sent for review, nor those supplied to the public libraries' (note at the end of the book). Production was in square 16mo., copies selling at 5 shillings. The large paper edition sold for ten shillings and sixpence. The book was published by Elkin Mathews and John Lane.

In the perspective which time allows us, we may see the Books of the Rhymers' Club as important evidence of a resurgence from the moribundity of much late nineteenth-century verse. Not for a long time had so many poets of real talent appeared upon the literary scene. The great Victorian poets had died, and with them the hitherto widely disseminated notion that poetry was a necessary adjunct to life, like religion, and that the poets' work deserved a place next to or near the Holy Bible. There was perhaps a feeling of relief among the hypocritical Philistines that there was no longer any poet with whom one had to 'keep up.' The school of Austin Dobson, Lang and Gosse had applied file and chisel to the fretting out of new verse forms but their poetry was essentially for the connoisseur. They had not attempted to lead the spirit into new realms of thought and feeling.

The Philistinism which most English poets have had to combat or disregard found a complacent voice, with which to greet the threat of new talent, in the following review of the *Book of the Rhymers' Club* which appeared as a fourth leader in the *Daily News* for Saturday, 20 February, 1892 (p. 5):

> Yet we can hardly say that poetry is out of fashion, when such vast quantities of poetry are written. It is the malady of not marking that we are suffering from. Nobody can catch the public ear. The public does not care for twilights, and Love and Death; the public has an especial aversion to sonnets. . . .

I shall omit most of the subsequent remarks in this vein. The writer goes on to accord grudging praise to Johnson but cannot for long keep his own ego suppressed:

> . . . Perhaps the best poem of the twelve is Mr. Johnson's, who has the courage to be a Royalist, and to hymn Charles I.
>
> *His soul was of the Saints,*
> *And Art to him was joy.*
>
> But the ghost of STRAFFORD is apt to disturb these loyal meditations. A song of Mr TODHUNTER'S would be more delightful if the first lines did not recall a song of Mr BROWNING'S in 'Paracelsus'. Then comes a poem on 'Beauty Accurst' [by Le Gallienne] a most unlucky type of beauty.
>
> *Toads kiss my feet, and creatures of the mire;*
> *The snails will leave their shells to watch me there.*
>
> The snail, like the oyster, may be crossed in love. Sleepy kine, too, behave in an unusual manner, 'and press their oozy lips over my hair'. Happily this is not a common kind of misfortune, though most irritating to the sufferer. 'I smite the ox, and crush the toad to death,' says the speaker, and we do not wonder at it.

A disadvantage of the collective form of publication is that, where the talents displayed are unequal, the reviewer (avid then, as sometimes now, for something which will enable him to display his wit) can damn the whole through the weaker parts. Thus, this reviewer's comments on 'Beauty Accurst' are, to me at least, amusing, and the casual reader would soon extend a derisive mood to the rest, particularly when some other poems gave excuse for the exercise of an outraged puritanism.

The Rhymers were unfortunate in those of their members who took it upon themselves to speak for the company as a whole.

G. A. Greene's 'Song of the Songsmiths' is poor doggerel of which the following is a fair sample:

[verse 2] *Who is it jeers at our song?*
Scoffs at an art sublime?
Who is it jeers at our song?
We who know right from wrong
Worship the godlike rhyme.

The Rhymers who seem to have had most in common, and these were the least talented ones, unfortunately succeed in suggesting a kind of literary heartiness by no means characteristic of a Yeats, Dowson, Johnson, or Symons. Ernest Rhys heads those Club members who seem bent upon a roystering fraternalism; 'The Toast' is an attempt to capture the Elizabethan spirit which is as little successful as Victorian Gothic architecture in summoning the atmosphere of the age under contribution. Rhys has another, different vein—the Celtic one. The unfamiliar mythology which this carries with it strikes chillingly, as is generally the case, at a first reading, and one requires convincing that the effort to grasp the personages and their symbolism, if any, is worthwhile. With Yeats the beauty of the verse is the stimulus to this. Yeats was, moreover, not delving into Irish legend in a merely antiquarian spirit but was convinced of its relevance to a new symbolism which would awaken men to something buried in a kind of collective national memory and imagination. Rhys's 'Howell the Tall' (in the *Second Book of the Rhymers' Club*) is, by comparison, a museum-piece. His ballad 'The Wedding of Pale Bronwen' is an effective exercise in the art of imitating old ballads. Good pastiche.

A poem such as Ernest Radford's 'Freedom in a Suburb' is a foretaste of the 'Georgian School' of verse in which the principal delusion was that a poetical subject or a fine or touching sentiment constitutes poetry—that there is no need to subject these to the discipline of art. It is interesting to compare with a poem of Johnson's, Radford's poem, in which sympathy is expressed with the London city worker who keeps his soul intact in his suburban home. Radford has a tender and new conception but cannot write verse; Johnson has consummate skill and often catches the elegiac note of a Gray or an Arnold but has really no new conceptions. Johnson's skilful mastery of verse forms has earned him the praise of more recent critics, Ezra Pound being perhaps the best known. Yeats praised Johnson's reading of his poem suggested 'By the Statue of King Charles at Charing Cross,' which appears in the first Rhymers' book. This is the most anthologized of Johnson's poems. It prompts me to Yeats's question: whether Francis Thompson thought 'what seemed to us simplicity, mere emptiness'. Its tonal effects when read aloud are striking but there is no attempt at economy of statement. Instead of the concentration often considered the chief characteristic distinguishing poetry from prose, Johnson obtains an effect by accumulation. One may consider the opening:

Sombre and rich, the skies;
Great glooms and starry plains.
Gently the night wind sighs;
Else a vast silence reigns.

There are six adjectives in only four short lines. There is one word which bears the chief emphasis in the verse. Is it the most significant? No, it is the word 'else.' Sense is subordinate to sound and the word 'else' has been employed as a musical stop, for the sake of alliteration and to hush the line into silence.

There *is* a technical mastery in this poem which makes the claim of several of Johnson's associates to be 'Rhymers' seem almost an impertinence:

The splendid silence clings
Around me: and around
The saddest of all kings
Crowned, and again discrowned.

This sounds magnificent, but really conveys very little. We have already been made aware of the vast silence in verse one. It is doubtful whether Johnson has anything really urgent to say. (A fuller consideration is given in my chapter on Johnson.)

Victor Plarr contributed one promising poem 'Epitaphium Citharistriae' which has a lightness of touch and sentiment recalling Herrick, but without his poignancy. 'To a Greek Gem,' which begins as musing of a rather obvious kind on the gem's history, declines from sober mediocrity into absurd quasi-Shakespearean grandiosity.

Yeats's contributions to the first book are all related to Ireland, chiefly to Irish folk-lore. His verses have a compression of thought and feeling and a vividness of imagery which expose by contrast the emptiness of a number of the other poems in the book. He has something definite to communicate and a great store-house of images such as that of the 'green branch hung with many a bell' which once restored the Irish people and which, in his 'Dedication of Irish Tales' he says his own poems are to resemble. 'The Lake Isle of Innisfree' was to become Yeats's most popular poem—however much he might later regret the fact. The strength and sincerity of the emotion expressed and the universality of this longing for a green place away from modern urban society constitute its intrinsic appeal. Yeats noted that he would not, at a later period, have used the archaic 'rise and go,' nor the inversions.

Two lines of Arthur Symons may illustrate the uncertainty of some of his 'impressionist' contributions:

The little amber-coloured dancers move,
Like little painted figures on a screen.
['Javanese Dancers']

In the collection of his *Poems*,[8] Symons has improved this to:

In measure while the gnats of music whirr,
The little amber-coloured dancers move,
Like painted idols seen to stir,
By the idolators in a magic grove.

T. W. Rolleston echoes the heartiness of Rhys, in his 'Ballade of the "Cheshire Cheese" In Fleet Street' from which these lines are typical:

The modern world, so stiff and stale,
You leave behind you when you please,
For long clay pipes and great old ale
And beefsteaks in the 'Cheshire Cheese'.

In the *Second Book of the Rhymers' Club*, Richard Le Gallienne continues to find inspiration in the nights of London, sharing in this the *métier* of Arthur Symons but with a moralizing strain in place of the latter's gay abandon and *mystique* of the curious. 'A Ballad of London' is an uneven poem which might have gained from extensive pruning. His second line is striking: 'Great flower that opens but at night,' but there is a suggestion of the precious in his description of street lamps as 'The iron lilies of the Strand.' The simile which begins his third verse is effective but his inspiration does not sustain him beyond this so that both matter and form limp to a close:

Like dragonflies, the hansoms hover,
With jewelled eyes, to catch the lover,
The streets are full of lights and loves,
Soft gowns and flutter of soiled doves.

In 'Ad Cinerarium,' Victor Plarr attempts a delicate sentiment and achieves its constant shadow, bathos:

Sure some mourner deemed immortal
What thou holdest and enfoldest,
Little house without a portal!
[The exclamation mark is his own.]

The same poet's 'Deer in Greenwich Park' begins interestingly by comparing the slum children with the animal occupants of the park, alike shadowy and furtive. What appears, however, to be a Davidson-like evocation of meaning and pathos in the naturalistic manner gives way to a 'Celtic' evocation of the ancestral memories of their wild past which the deer recall at night—an outcome which seems to me somewhat forced.

Yeats's contributions are of a piece with those which he made to the first book. 'The Rose in My Heart,' however, introduces a new symbol to which he was to return repeatedly for a time and to which his love for Maud Gonne seems to have been at least partly contributory.

T. W. Rolleston's 'Cycling Song' is Kiplingesque in rhythm, if not in subject matter:

In the airy whirling wheel is the springing strength of steel
And the sinew grows to steel day by day,
Till you feel your pulses leap at the easy swing and sweep
As the hedges flicker past upon the way.

He has got off to a good start, but bathos lurks round every corner:

And you never would have guessed how delicious is the rest
In the shade by the wayside inn, . . .

Barrack-Room Ballads had appeared in 1892 and Rolleston comes nearer to the spirit of Kipling in 'Noon-Day Elegiacs':

Something remains upon earth to be done,
to be dared, to be sought for,
Up with the anchor again! out with the sails
to the blast!
Out to the shock of the seas that encircle
the Fortunate Islands,
Vision and promise and prize, home of the
Wind of the Spring.

Johnson's poem 'The Dark Angel' has the emotional force of personally felt experience the lack of which I regretted in certain of his poems.

Yeats commented, in his article for the *Boston Pilot*, on the Rhymers' 'search for new subject matter'. It is a pity that Davidson, who more than any other Rhymer succeeded in finding material for poetry in the urban scene, refused to contribute to the books. Nevertheless the books provide ample evidence, then much needed, of the survival of the poetic spirit into an age of industrialism and materialism where the landscape is often urban or suburban.

The contributions which, to my mind, have the most striking breath of originality are not, however, in any sense an advance into new territory. I refer to the poems of Ernest Dowson. These convey that thrill of the blood which, when criticism has said its last word, still seems to me the ultimate seal of a true lyrical inspiration. I shall treat of Dowson more critically in the chapter on the poet, but I intend to quote here the whole of 'Amor Umbratilis' (from the first *Book of the Rhymers' Club*). It is the poem which, published in the *Hobby Horse*, seems to have first made people aware of Dowson's talent. It is quintessential Dowson—delicate, musical, sad, the poet of *lacrimae rerum:*

AMOR UMBRATILIS

A Gift of silence, Sweet!
Who may not ever hear:
To lay down at your unobservant feet,
Is all the gift I bear.
I have no songs to sing,
That you should heed or know;
I have no lilies, in full hands, to fling,
Across the path you go.
I cast my flowers away,
Blossoms unmeet for you:
The garland, I have gathered, in my day;
My rose-mary and rue.
I watch you pass and pass,
Serene and cold: I lay
My lips upon your trodden, daisied grass,
And turn my life away.
Yea, for I cast you, Sweet!
This one gift, you shall take:
Like ointment, on your unobservant feet,
My silence, for your sake.

We have seen two examples of the journalistic reception of the Rhymers. The *Daily Chronicle* reviewer is of that extremely common Victorian kind, the hearty, jolly, 'clubbable' man. His chief delight is apparently in his notion of the Rhymers' Club as a red-blooded, beef-eating fraternity. The jocular note, and dearth of real critical observation is as evident in a review by one of the Rhymers themselves, Richard Le Gallienne. His review was pseudonymously contributed to the *Star* for Thursday, 11 February, 1892:

> Because one happens to be a humble participator in an important event, is one necessarily to forego all reference to it? Is it possible that I can write this column this week just as though no 'Book of the Rhymers' Club' (Elkin Mathews) had come into the world, just because among the twelve (who have distilled their young lives into this volume) one happens to bear a name which may not be mentioned here? I read my duty other-

wise, and so, if it please you, intend to gossip of this 'gracious coronal of song', as though it had been woven but by eleven hands; an act really, as you will imagine, of some self-sacrifice, and for which I shall expect a more enduring crown of glory. The little book calls for no 'illuminated' explanations of its raison d'etre. By means of a neat preliminary 'toast' by Mr. Ernest Rhys, a capital 'Ballad of the Cheshire Cheese' by Mr. T. W. Rolleston, and an epilogue by Mr. G. A. Greene, it explains itself. These twelve—I beg your pardon, these eleven—rhymers are evidently a secret, an open secret, society of so-called though not *soi-disant*, 'minor' poets, who from time to time, like the morning stars, sing together at a well-known

'House of antique ease
Within the smoky city's pale.'

[The author then quotes from 'As once Rare Ben . . .' to 'ass of time'. (See above p. 28)]

. . . But these rhymers would appear to thus sit in the seat of their dead masters in no spirit but that of reverent discipleship. Were Herrick or Ben to pop in upon them, you would find them all on their feet in an instant, and not a rhyme amongst them. At least, I think so. Indeed, the modest, common-sense note of this book strikes one at once. It is an evil time for rhyme, say these lyric spirits; we know we bring no mighty line, but is that any reason why we shouldn't chirp out the best we've got? So, like antique gentlemen, these rhymers have chirped in their cups, and this 'Book' is the essence of their *noctes*.

When eleven heads collaborate to fill ninety pages, they must indeed be sheep's heads if they cannot do it respectably. And it might, at any rate, seem likely that a book into which eleven had put their best would be a better book than anyone of them could do single-voiced. Mathematically, it should be eleven times as good. But then, verse eleven times as good as some of these poems would bid fair

'To o'ertop old Pelion, or the skyish head
Of blue Olympus.'

The poems I am thinking of especially are Mr. Lionel Johnson's 'By the Statue of King Charles at Charing Cross', Mr. W. B. Yeats' 'Father Gilligan', Mr. Ernest Radford's 'Love and Death', and Mr. Arthur Symons' 'A Death in the Forest'. How unhappy Mr. Johnson must have been made by the new electrical monstrosity we have just seen 'Jet upward in the midday blossom', like some iron upas, hard by that sacred statue:

[The 'King Charles' poem is then quoted.]

One has often wondered whether Charles was worthy of all the good blood spilt on his behalf; but one is quite certain that he was unworthy of such good rhyme, rhyme of such an austere dignity as this.

I quote Mr. Johnson because this is his first attempt to win his spurs as a poet. Mr. Yeats, 'the man who dreams of fairyland', by his 'Wanderings of Oisin', Mr. Radford by his 'Chambers Twain', Mr. Symons by his 'Days and Nights', have each individualized themselves in the minds of that 'little clan' who care about poetry, and so each can afford to be generous to a new comer. Yet it is a pity for you to miss Mr. Yeats' ballad, a ballad imaginative as Coleridge and Miss Rossetti's only are imaginative; then Mr. Radford's apologue is so neat, and Mr. Symons' 'Death in the Forest' is so passionate. If we are to judge by the latter, the attitude of the *fin-de-siècle* man to his woman fellow-sinner is far more generous than we should have thought:

'We sinned, but it is I who pay the price:
I say that she shall dwell in Paradise.
For me the feast in hell is on the board.
Ah, not the woman, not the woman, Lord.'

This is better than 'the woman gave unto me, and I did eat', which we would have expected from him.

On this subject of the blessed apple, by the way, Mr. Edwin J. Ellis has a fine poem, 'New Words and Old', and among the remaining good things I notice Mr. Ernest Dowson's 'Carmelite Nuns', which I had the pleasure of welcoming on its first appearance in the pages of *The Hobby Horse.*

One thing strikes us favourably—the general English character of the book; also the absence of affectation. These poems, whatever their value, rely for it entirely on their poetry, and not on tricks of style, or mere eccentricity of fancy. Such as Musset's image of the moon above a church steeple, which has become the type of all such pseudo-originality:

Et c'est, dans la nuit brune,
Sur son clocher jauni,
La lune
Comme un point sur un i.[9]

Le Gallienne's pseudonym in the *Star* of 'Log-roller' is more a proudly defiant than guilty admission. He was convinced of the importance of the writers whom he encountered as John Lane's reader and in his personal life and had therefore no hesitation in using any platform from which to proclaim it. Indeed, Le Gallienne's principal importance in the period seems to have been as a discoverer of talent and middleman for it to the new reading public. In this light, the jolly, popular nature of the preceding review has its justification.

Le Gallienne's closing approbation of 'the general English character of the book' is typical, and distances him from Rhymers such as Dowson, Symons and even the Yeats of a year or two later. All of these, and many of those whose works John Lane published, were very susceptible to influences from France. Le Gallienne consistently shrank from what was, and is, often referred to as the Decadence. The following poem, from his *English Poems* (London, 1892), shows how closely aligned he was with the John Bullish school which was to start rampaging in the year of Wilde's trial:

TO THE READER

Art was a palace once, things great and fair
And strong and holy, found a temple there;
Now 'tis a lazar-house of leprous men!
O shall we never hear an English song again!
Still English larks mount in the merry morn,
An English May still brings an English thorn,
Still English daises up and down the grass,
Still English love for English lad and lass—
Yet youngsters blush to sing an English song.

Thou nightingale that for six hundred years
Sang to the world—O art thou husht at last!
For, not of thee this new voice in our ears,
Music of France that once was of the spheres;
And not of thee these strange green flowers that spring
From daisy roots and seem to bear a sting.

The Picture of Dorian Gray had appeared in 1891 and it is possible that Le Gallienne has something of this kind in mind. It will be remembered that that novel involves a strange French book (Huysmans' *A Rebours*, probably). 'Green' was associated with decadence before 'yellow', as, for example, in Hichens' satire on Wilde, *The Green Carnation.* This was probably through a series of associations ranging from crème de menthe to the favourite colours of certain French impressionist painters. The two colours are linked in Gilbert and Sullivan's:

'*Greenery-yallery,*
Grosvenor Gallery,
foot-in-the-grave young man.'
[*Patience* (London, 1888).]

It is ironical that Le Gallienne's dandyish style of dressing (which Max Beerbohm caricatured) was thought, by many literary men with whom he was unpopular, to be an imitation of Wilde's.

On the *Star*, where he had succeeded Clement Shorter as literary critic, he was in the company of 'Corno di Bassetto' (Bernard Shaw, the music critic), A. B. Walkley (drama) and Joseph Pennell (art). Grant Richards wrote of him:

> He was, as a critic, first and foremost, a stimulus to the enjoyment of letters, and it is certain that if his scholarship was neither wide nor deep (and indeed he would have been the last to suggest that it was) his love of books was something that lay far deeper than scholarship.[10]

As John Lane's reader, it was Le Gallienne who brought John Davidson to light, through *Fleet Street Eclogues* (London, 1893).

Intelligent comment on the *Book of the Rhymers' Club* appeared in an article in the *Church Quarterly*, XXXV, 201, of October, 1892. It treats of poetry by Bridges, Mackail, J. B. B. Nichols and H. C. Beeching, and then of the *Book of the Rhymers' Club*. The writer provides a summary of English literary history with the point that England, in the early 'nineties, is at one of the pauses which always follow great work. (In a footnote the late news of Tennyson's death is recorded.)

> Browning, Matthew Arnold, Clough, Mrs. Browning, Rossetti, Newman are gone; Swinburne and William Morris have given us their best work, and no new poet has arisen yet to take their place. We have reached the inevitable period of decay, of pause, and, as it were, of marking time . . .

Of the *Book of the Rhymers' Club*, the reviewer writes:

> We may be mistaken, but several of the writers impress one as being earnestly devoted to literature, a devotion which should bear good fruit, though not necessarily in verse, hereafter. The writing of verse is a good apprenticeship to the composition of literary prose, and it may be that more than one of these young authors will do their best work outside the trammels of metre. The verse-work is good, the thoughts generally true and occasionally somewhat new, and the language usually natural, poetical, and unexaggerated: the latter a feature especially remarkable in youthful and inevitably self-conscious work. At the same time there is nothing in the volume which contains any definite promise, or more than the mere possibility, of great poetic achievement in the future. The lessons of past literature have been learned; there is much earnestness, probably much real pains, but the note of distinction, of originality, is wanting.

> The scale, moreover, is very small; it is cameo-carving, not sculpture, and in a great work of art, as Aristotle taught long ago, the element of size must not be absent. It may be said that these are but preludings, specimens of the self-training in composition by which the poet, however great his natural genius, must learn his trade. But we doubt very much whether these writers are below the age at which great poets have generally shown some real and decisive promise of great work. . . .
> . . . One feature is worth noticing, which is characteristic of most of the poetry of to-day, and which marks the larger, and certainly the better, portion of the poems of this volume. This is the gravity of tone which pervades them, a gravity which is distinct from the seriousness of poetic purpose already noted, and belongs to the thought rather than to the style. A light and only half-serious manner has generally been characteristic of young poets; the emotions expressed might be passionate enough, but they were understood not to be more than skin-deep. The young poets of to-day seem to be imbued with a seriousness which is not, as might reasonably be suspected, mere affectation. Neither is it pessimism, which is almost always affectation, except when it is indigestion. It is simply a habit of thinking seriously, of allowing the mind to dwell upon grave topics. Of course there is sometimes exaggeration, sometimes even insincerity in this seriousness, the former, at any rate, being the natural concomitant of immaturity; but the basis of it is sincere and genuine. It is partly an inheritance from Matthew Arnold, partly the result of the same causes that produced it in Matthew Arnold himself. The conditions of modern life are serious enough. Serious thoughts, in philosophy, in politics, in social matters, in religion, surround us all from schooldays onward. Some minds pass them over, some play with them because they are fashionable, some are touched by them, it may be lightly, it may be deeply. But even a light acquaintance with them, if it be genuine, may be sufficient to colour poetry; and this will account for the general tone of contemporary verse, where there are no special circumstances . . . to justify a real melancholy.

Reviews of the *Second Book of the Rhymers' Club* are harder to come by. On 26 June, 1894, W. B. Yeats wrote from his home in Bedford Park to John O'Leary:

> . . . I send you *The Second Book of the Rhymers' Club* in which everybody is tolerably good except the Trinity College men, Rolleston, Hillier, Todhunter and Greene, who are intolerably bad as was to be expected—Todhunter is of course skilful enough with more matter of fact themes and quite admits the

dreadful burden of the T.C.D.[11] tradition—and some are exceedingly good, notably Plarr, Dowson, Johnson and Le Gallienne.[12]

The following review of *The Second Book of The Rhymers' Club* appeared in the *Athenaeum*, 25 August, 1894:

Just as in the sister art of painting, the public seek the exhibitions of the New English Art Club to see what the members of our younger school are about, so in the collected verses of the Rhymers' Club may possibly be found some indications of the future of British poetry. We cannot profess to be in love with the tendency towards co-operative production which is displayed by both the bodies we have mentioned, holding as we do that the strongest work is always done by those who stand apart from all such coteries and shun the mutual admiration they are too apt to engender. But having said so much we are glad to be able to bestow unstinted praise upon certain portions, at all events, of the poetical manifesto of the Rhymers. Mr. W. B. Yeats, to mention one of the best of the collaborators, is something more than a mere versifier, and he has seldom been seen to more advantage than in 'The Folk of the Air' and 'The Cap and Bells'. His graceful method is also well shown in 'The Rose in my Heart', which we make no excuse for printing in full. [The poem follows] . . . The verse of Mr. Ernest Rhys is most successful when it deals with the themes of Welsh antiquity, and the longest of his poems in the collection, entitled 'Howell the Tall', is a favourable specimen of his powers. Mr. Arthur Symons and Mr. Ernest Dowson evince their customary disposition of dwelling upon the less wholesome aspects of life in such verses as those which they call respectively 'A Variation upon Love' and 'Non sum qualis eram bonae sub regno Cynarae'. Of Mr. Richard Le Gallienne's contributions to the ἔρανος, such as 'A Ballad of London' and 'Time's Monotone', it is enough to say that they exhibit a certain undisciplined vigour, but are wanting in distinction and finish. To none of all the band of bardlings may the *limae labor* be more strongly commended than to this clever yet unequal writer, who seems indeed to be discovering his truer vocation in the region of prose. When we return to the work of Mr. Lionel Johnson, we discover a delicate fancy and a considerable facility for its expression. 'Mystic and Cavalier' is good, but 'To Morfydd' is better—in some respects, perhaps, the best thing in the whole book, with its curious haunting refrain. [The poem follows.]
. . . We must hurry over the remainder of the poetic company. Mr. John Todhunter is in evidence with some creditable verses on the funeral of the late Laureate, and (among other

things) a 'Euthanasia' upon the pagan sentiments of which we cannot honestly congratulate him. There are also some careful, if slightly affected bits of craftsmanship from Mr. Victor Plarr and Mr. Ernest Radford; while the most noticeable effort of Mr. T. W. Rolleston is his vivacious 'Cycling Song', which strikes a welcome note of realism among the otherwise somewhat indefinite harmonies of this slim green volume. Mr. Arthur Cecil Hillier adds a few pleasant poems to the general sum total, which is not materially affected, for better or worse, by the laborious lispings of Mr. Edwin J. Ellis and Mr. G. A. Greene.

As we have seen, the Rhymers' Club comprehended a great variety not only of poetic styles and interests but also of influence and tendencies. It would be convenient if one could say that it represented the best that was being thought and done in the realms of verse in the 1890s but to say this would be to ignore the Henley, Kipling, Newbolt group of 'men of action' as also the more secluded spirits such as Bridges, Patmore and Housman. Of all the Rhymers, Yeats, as we have seen and will note further, had the widest contacts with all kinds of literary men and we shall see how others of the Rhymers had their particular circles tangential to or removed from the Rhymers' Club itself. Rather than attempt those often misleading and never very accurate groupings of writers under such labels as 'Celtic', 'Symbolist', 'Decadent' and so forth, I have sought, in the chapters which follow, to devote fuller consideration to those Rhymers whom I consider to be of most interest. By a study of each of these in turn, in their relations with other Rhymers' Club members, and to some extent in their other fields of activity, the picture of the Club which I have already sketched will, I hope, be filled out in some detail.

REFERENCES

[1] *Autobiographies*, p. 301.

[2] Rhys, *Letters from Limbo*, p. 71.

[3] *The Letters of Ernest Dowson*, ed. Desmond Flower and Henry Maas (London, 1967), pp. 202–203. Manmohan Ghose (1869–1924) was a student at Christ Church, Oxford, in the late 1880s, with Stephen Phillips and Laurence Binyon. He published a book of verse, *Primavera*, in 1890.

[4] Longaker, p. 101. Image's notice appeared in the *Church Reformer*, XI (March 1892) and opposed Lang's view that the small number of copies published was a sign of weakness. It was, Image countered, a mark of 'the modest temper of the Club'.

[5] The final poem of the book, this one of Greene's, is printed in italics as is the first one, by Rhys.

[6] *The Letters of W. B. Yeats*, p. 474.

[7] Le Gallienne, p. 183.

[8] Arthur Symons, *Poems* (London, 1906).

[9] Musset's poem should read: *C'était, dans la nuit brune,*
Sur le clocher jauni, . . .

[10] Grant Richards, *Author Hunting* (New York, 1934), p. 83.

[11] Trinity College, Dublin.

[12] *The Letters of W. B. Yeats*, p. 232.

CHAPTER IV

William Butler Yeats: 1890-1896

Poets with whom I learned my trade,
Companions of the Cheshire Cheese, . . .

(W. B. YEATS, 'The Grey Rock')

THE trio which founded the Rhymers' Club was Celtic: a Welshman, Rhys, and two Irishmen, Yeats and Rolleston. As their numbers increased the Celtic element also increased so that we find Jepson describing them as *all* 'very Celtic', a humorous comment on their inclinations rather than their pedigrees as far, at least, as Johnson and, particularly, Dowson were concerned—the latter was 'inclined to believe that there was a Celtic strain in him.' Johnson at one time assumed a brogue and addressed Jepson as 'Me dearr'. Celts indeed were John Todhunter, Plarr (his father an Alsatian), Symons and Yeats. Jepson says Yeats 'who was plainly a Firbolg, was the most Celtic of all, and they all declared that there was a Celtic Renaissance.'[1] He could also have included Ellis, Hillier and Rolleston in his list of Celts. Most of the specifically 'Celtic' activities of Yeats, Rolleston, Todhunter, and Lionel Johnson took place outside the Rhymers' Club movement itself. A Celtic renaissance was taking place but it was not really apparent in any of the Celtic Rhymers besides Yeats. E. A. Boyd points out that the chief work of the older Irish poets of the Club had been shaped by the English tradition, that which Yeats described (above, p. 42) as 'the dreadful T.C.D. tradition'. They were, of course, inspired by the propaganda of Yeats and supported the renaissance movement, but the general tone of their work did not fundamentally alter. Johnson was so much a product of English birth and Oxford education that he was in a similar position to his older Irish friends who 'could but partially recapture the tradition which had been reborn to displace in Irish literature the tradition in which they had developed.'[2] Yeats alone was Irish through and through and this is apparent from all of his poems in the books of the Rhymers' Club. The other Irish contributions, with the exception of Johnson's *Celtic Speech*, do not reveal specifically national characteristics.

The Club, however, was above all intent upon the craft of verse itself—a verse which was to be free from the 'impurities' of politics, science, religion and rhetoric. It would appear that in the years 1891 to 1896, the increase in Yeats's practical organizing activities concerned with a new Irish literature was matched by a decline in the specifically Irish purport of his poetry. In November, 1891, Yeats wrote to O'Leary: '... Lionel Johnson who is an Irishman talks of being in Ireland next Spring and of lecturing if we like to the Young Ireland League or to our Dublin Social and Literary Club. Rhys also has intentions of turning up ...'[3]

Rhys did not turn up but Johnson did. The latter's 'Irishness' was really somewhat tenuous. Boyd wrote:

> The Irish strain in his blood was of the slightest, and a generation or two of highly Anglicized forbears, one of whom helped to crush the rebellion in 1798, did not tend to strengthen his sense of Irish nationality.[4]

Johnson was an 'Irishman' in the same way that he was a Roman Catholic and a Jacobite—he was an intellectual convert.

It is not, of course, my purpose here to follow out the course of Yeats's multifarious activities. But we must not altogether overlook that active life which engaged him even throughout his most 'aesthetic years' when the Rhymers flourished—the active life which was to be his refuge and salvation from the tragic ends which beset so many of his fellow Rhymers and their associates.

In a letter to Katharine Tynan during July, 1891, Yeats attributes 'a certain amount of influence with reviewers' to the Rhymers' Club and suggests that he will probably be able to mention her work in: the *Boston Pilot*, *Anti-Jacobin*, *Star*, *Pall Mall*, *Queen*, and *Speaker*, the last of whose reviews are 'very much in the friendly hand of John Davidson.' (*Letters*, p. 172.)

Yeats's collaboration with Edwin Ellis in the compiling of an edition of Blake was not for monetary reward. The publisher, Bernard Quaritch, paid its compilers with free copies of the work and of the prints included in it. The work was begun in February, 1889 (*Letters*, p. 122) and was a constant concern until it appeared in 1893 in three volumes instead of the projected two, and entitled the *Works of William Blake*, 'with a memoir and interpretation by Edwin John Ellis and W. B. Yeats.' In his own copy, Yeats wrote:

> The writing of this book is mainly Ellis's, the thinking is as much mine as his. The biography is by him. He re-wrote and trebled in size a biography of mine. The greater part of the 'symbolic system' is my writing; the rest of the book was written by Ellis working over short accounts of the books by me, except in the case of the 'literary period' the account of the minor poems, and the account of Blake's art theories which are all his own except in so far as we discussed everything together.[5]

The collaboration with Ellis had its problems: 'Ellis is magnificent within his limits,' Yeats wrote to O'Leary, 'but threatens to overthrow them, and beyond them he is useless through lack of mystical knowledge . . .' (*Letters*, p. 163). Then a difficulty with Mrs. Ellis caused her to refuse to have Yeats in her house for a time. 'She got the curious delusion that I had some mesmeric power over her that made her ill. The sight of me made her grow white with terror. She has now got over the delusion and wants me to go there again but I am afraid of its returning and so stay away.' (*Letters*, p. 164.) The constant preoccupation with Blake strongly influenced Yeats's imagination and style. It reinforced his belief that religious truth lay hidden in symbol and encouraged the tendency, already evident in *The Wanderings of Oisin*, towards hermetic as compared with popular writing. He had written to Katharine Tynan, concerning the second part of *Oisin*, that he had there said, under the disguise of symbolism, several things to which he alone had the key. The readers were to find the romance but not the symbol. 'If they did, it would spoil the art. Yet the whole poem is full of symbols—if it be full of ought but clouds.' (*Letters*, p. 88.)

Nevertheless, Yeats continued to write also in a popular style and to vacillate between the obscurely symbolic and the popular.

> When he began writing he hurled himself away in pursuit of the shades of Spenser and Shelley; then veered in the opposite direction hunting after local legends, ballads, and fairies; became aware of more important and wider fields to be explored with 'The Wanderings of Oisin' and its few secret symbols; then hankered after Innisfree and Faeryland once more with deeper longing strengthened by his city-dwelling; again sought broader Irish themes with an increasing interest in European symbolism.[6]

By 1892, when *The Countess Kathleen and Various Legends and Lyrics* was published, we find an increasing complexity in his symbolic verse, particularly in the 'Rose' poems included there.

In many of the poems there is a new note of spare vigour contrasting with the dream-heavy passages of 'Oisin'. In 'The Rose of the World', for example:

Who dreamed that beauty passes like a dream?
For these red lips, with all their mournful pride,
Mournful that no new wonder may betide,
Troy passed away in one high funeral gleam,
And Usna's children died.

The simpler poems in this collection were nearly all written earlier, 1889 to 1890.[7] The influence of Yeats's Blake studies is apparent in such verses as:

And God would bid his warfare cease,
Saying all things were well;
And softly make a rosy peace,
A peace of Heaven and Hell. ['The Rose of Peace'.]

The significance of the Rose symbol in Yeats's poetry developed from a relatively simple and popular conception of love to something more complex and elusive. In the 1892 edition of *The Countess Kathleen*, Yeats commented that the rose was a favourite symbol with the Irish poets, not only for love but also for Ireland, as in de Vere's line 'The little black rose shall be red at last' and in Mangan's 'Dark Rosaleen'. Such a limited, nationalist symbol was alien to Yeats's far broader purpose but it is evident at this stage in his writing that the Rose is, in fact, an unknown quantity and that it is easier to state what it is not than what it is. The approach to the full revelation of the symbol is in itself a poetical task, and the revelation a poetical experience. Yeats's later attempts at prose explanation can, however, be of some help. In a note dated 1925, for instance, he observes that the Rose differs from the Intellectual Beauty of Shelley and of Spenser 'in that I have imagined it as suffering with man and not as something pursued and seen from far.'[8] The Rose had to unfold itself; invisible gates had to open, as they had opened for Blake, Swedenborg and Boehme. In a seemingly disintegrated cosmos, the poet might still find his way to a universal myth, to the springs of the collective unconscious through an imaginative literature which,

> though made by many minds would seem the work of a single mind, and turn our places of beauty or legendary association into holy symbols. . . .
>
> . . . I thought that for a time I could rhyme of love, calling it *The Rose*, because of the Rose's double meaning; of a fisherman who had 'never a crack' in his heart; of an old woman complaining of the idleness of the young, or of some cheerful

fiddler, all those things that 'popular poets' write of, but that I must some day—on that day when the gates began to open—become difficult or obscure. With a rhythm that still echoed Morris I prayed to the Red Rose, to Intellectual Beauty:—

Come near, come near, come near—Ah, leave me still
A little space for the rose-breath to fill!
Lest I no more hear common things . . .
But seek alone to hear the strange things said
By God to the bright hearts of those long dead,
And learn to chaunt a tongue men do not know.[9]

Yeats's association with the Rhymers was to confirm him in his sense that he must 'become difficult or obscure' and to make it increasingly difficult for him to 'hear common things'.

The Rhymer who seems to have influenced Yeats most at the beginning is Lionel Johnson who himself, in conjunction with Arthur Symons, brought to bear on the Rhymers the influence of Walter Pater. Yeats considered, in retrospect, that Rossetti had probably been the most powerful subconscious influence on the Rhymers but that for their 'philosophy' they looked consciously to Pater. *Marius the Epicurean* seemed to Yeats 'the only great prose in modern English' but he wondered whether the attitude of mind which it encouraged had led some of the Rhymers to disastrous experiments with life. 'It taught us to walk upon a rope, tightly stretched through serene air, and we were left to keep our feet upon a swaying rope in a storm.' It does not seem to me that there is much vital connection between Pater's influence and what Yeats goes on to say of Dowson's 'breaking his heart for the daughter of the keeper of an Italian eating house in dissipation and drink'; Dowson was undoubtedly very susceptible to certain aspects of the Zeitgeist, but as well blame Mürger's *Vie de Bohème* (which delighted Dowson at Oxford), or Baudelaire, or half a dozen others. Johnson's life, I would say, took a far greater impression from Pater's—for good and ill. Yeats remarks, in the same passage from *Autobiographies* to which I have been alluding,[10] that Pater made the Rhymers learned and ceremonious, polite and distant in their relations with one another. This was a direct consequence of a respect for tradition which made them claim the whole past of literature for their authority. In a way, one may see in these comments the reaction of the 'provincial' Yeats to the Oxford men—his comments on the Rhymers' ways of dressing, noted earlier, are of a piece with these. Johnson and Symons maintained communication with Oxford, particularly with their 'sage'. Johnson told Yeats that he had noticed books on political economy in Pater's rooms and that the latter had remarked, 'Everything that has occupied man, for any length of time, is worthy of our study.'

Yeats admits that Johnson's reports were not always to be trusted, and in this case it is worth remarking that this dictum of the sage could have been *read* by both Yeats and Johnson (and probably was) in the chapter 'Pico Della Mirandola' of Pater's *Renaissance* (London, 1873)[11] where it, or something very similar, is twice expressed in the form: '. . . its generous belief that nothing which had ever interested the human mind could wholly lose its vitality.'

To Yeats, Johnson represented the academic tradition which he knew himself to lack. As a poet, of course, Johnson belonged to the classical school, which was inimical to Yeats, but it was a classicism filtered through Arnold and Pater, investing the poet with the role of a priest and elevating art to a sacrosanct, hieratic level. Moreover, Yeats's objection to the classical school was tempered with that reverence for tradition which the Rhymers encouraged. In connection with the Irish movement, Johnson's Roman Catholicism was useful to Yeats in carrying the support of the Irish Catholics while his reputed learning in theology could be employed to forestall opponents of the new Irish literature who sniffed for heresies.

As Yeats indicated, the influence of Pater was not merely literary but extended into day-to-day deportment and conduct. To it is largely attributable the 'solemnity' which the various commentators quoted in my earlier chapters had noted at the Rhymers' gatherings, as also the intended sobriety of dress. When Katharine Tynan called on Yeats in 1893 for an interview for the *Sketch* '. . . she found him changed. He had learnt to assume a dignity and courtliness of manner that gained in sincerity and strength with later years. He turned to a more artificial concept of what a poet should be. He could exclude much of his life from his poetry because of this ability to conform to a chosen pattern. The pattern was one of "pure" poetry. . . .'[12]

In a radio broadcast on the 11th of October, 1936, Yeats commented on the general attitude to life and art of the *Rhymers:*

> A church in the style of Inigo Jones opens on to a grass lawn a few hundred yards from the Marble Arch. It was designed by a member of the Rhymers' Club whose architecture, like his poetry, seemed to exist less for its own sake than to illustrate his genius as a connoisseur. I have sometimes thought that masterpiece, perhaps the smallest church in London, the most appropriate symbol of all that was most characteristic in the art of my friends. Their poems seemed to say: 'You will remember us the longer because we are very small, very unambitious.' Yet my friends were most ambitious men; they wished to express life at its intense moments, those moments that are brief because of their intensity, and at those moments

> alone. In the Victorian era the most famous poetry was often a passage in a poem of some length, perhaps of great length, a poem full of thoughts that might have been expressed in prose. A short lyric seemed an accident, an interruption amid more serious work. Somebody has quoted Browning as saying that he could have written many lyrics had he thought them worth the trouble. The aim of my friends, my own aim, if it sometimes made us prefer the acorn to the oak, the small to the great, freed us from many things that we thought an impurity. Swinburne, Tennyson, Arnold, Browning, had admitted so much psychology, science, moral fervour. Had not Verlaine said of 'In Memoriam', 'when he should have been broken-hearted he had many reminiscences'. We tried to write like the poets of the Greek Anthology, or like Catullus, or like the Jacobean Lyrists, men who wrote while poetry was still pure. We did not look forward or look outward, we left that to the prose writers; we looked back. We thought it was in the very nature of poetry to look back, to resemble those Swedenborgian angels who are described as moving forever towards the day-spring of their youth. In this we were all, orderly and disorderly alike, in full agreement. . . .
>
> . . . We, too, thought always that style should be proud of its ancestry, of its traditional high breeding, that an ostentatious originality was out of place whether in the arts or in good manners.
>
> . . . My generation, because it disliked Victorian rhetorical, moral fervour, came to dislike all rhetoric.[13]

Many of the interests which Yeats mentions here—the Greek Anthology, Catullus, the Jacobean Lyrists—were acquired by him from the other Rhymers. His opposition to rhetoric was not particularly strong before his association with the group but after this, as Louis MacNeice wrote, 'It was to be a long time before Yeats stopped throttling the rhetorician inside himself.'[14]

When Johnson began to succumb to alcohol in 1895, Yeats found it impossible to maintain his close friendship with him. To do so meant providing him with drink or joining with him in its pursuit.[15] Late in the same year Yeats moved from Bedford Park into rooms adjoining those of Arthur Symons in Fountain Court in the Temple. Their usual occupant was away, so they made an attractive, convenient and free *pied-à-terre* for Yeats who was now so often away in Ireland that a more permanent residence would have involved wasteful expense.

Symons was no less a disciple of Pater than Johnson though his poetry was vastly different from Johnson's and rather despised by him. He was primarily a critic, with a style like Pater's, and he was very much occupied, at this time, with making known to his English readers the literature of contemporary France—a process begun by Matthew Arnold and continued in the 'eighties, in a very different manner, by George Moore. Yeats was as much influenced by Symons as he was by Johnson, and their association continued till 1908. Yeats wrote: 'At first I was repelled by Symons because, with a superficial deduction, I suppose, from the chapter in Marius "Animula Vagula", . . . he saw nothing in literature but a source of impassioned philosophy.'[16] Then he discovered in him a remarkable mental sympathy and capacity for entering the thoughts of another and enriching them. Symons read him passages from Verlaine and Mallarmé and thereby deepened his longing for the 'sacred book' which would 'open the doors'. Yeats's knowledge of French was small, but he struggled through Villiers de l'Isle-Adam's *Axël*, feeling at the time that this was indeed such a book, an experience which he had known several times before, beginning, in boyhood, with Shelley's *Prometheus Unbound*. It seemed to Yeats, in retrospect, that he and Symons extracted a constant intensity from life by way of literature, whether the literature concerned was the Song of Songs or the Sermon on the Mount. Symons was making metrical translations of Verlaine, Calderón, Saint John of the Cross and Mallarmé and Yeats considered that those of Mallarmé 'may have given elaborate form to my verses of those years, to the latter poems of *The Wind Among the Reeds*, to *The Shadowy Waters*, while Villiers de l'Isle-Adam had shaped whatever in my *Rosa Alchemica* Pater had not shaped.' Yeats particularly remembered Symons first reading to him, in Fountain Court, Mallarmé's poem, 'Herodiade's address to some Sibyl who is her nurse and, it may be, the moon also':

The horror of my virginity
Delights me, and I would envelop me
In the terror of my tresses, that, by night,
Inviolate reptile, I might feel the white
And glimmering radiance of thy frozen fire,
Thou that art chaste and diest of desire,
White night of ice and of the cruel snow!
Eternal sister, my lone sister, lo
My dreams uplifted before thee! now, apart,
So rare a crystal is my dreaming heart,
And all about me lives but in mine own
Image, the idolatrous mirror of my pride,
Mirroring this Herodiade diamond-eyed.

[*Autobiographies*, pp. 319–321.]

By April 1896 Yeats had left Fountain Court and established himself in rooms at 18, Woburn Buildings,[17] a passage near the intersection of Upper Woburn Place with the Euston Road. He had been introduced to 'Diana Vernon,' Mrs. Olivia Shakespear, by her cousin Lionel Johnson. She was the wife of a solicitor much older than herself.[18] In her company Yeats tried to console himself for his misery over Maud Gonne's refusal to marry him. The liaison appears to have been brief and to have inspired two of the poems in *The Wind Among the Reeds*, 'Michael Robartes bids his beloved be at Peace' and 'The Travail of Passion'. The years 1893–1898 were the time in which Yeats's most complex and esoteric work was produced. *The Wind Among the Reeds* (1889), comprising the poems of these years, and *Rosa Alchemica* (1896), which is a fantastic story, demonstrate that what Yeats had prognosticated concerning his poetry—that he 'must some day—on that day when the gates began to open—become difficult or obscure. . . .' had indeed come to pass. Whether the gates had begun to open seemed doubtful even then. Jeffares writes:

> He was worried over his work. It seemed that he had lost his old emotions which were rooted in the countryside. His poems were becoming over-elaborate and slow-moving. He had written 'Rosa Alchemica' which was in its complexity a long way from the simplicity of the essays of *The Celtic Twilight*. This new work was not likely to help the revival of imaginative writing in Ireland. And he wondered if, after all his love of the Irish scenery, he was really to write an elaborate mysticism without any special birthplace.[19]

The worry over his work was paralleled by his emotional unhappiness. Jeffares (p. 107) quotes from 'unpublished material':

> I saw much now of Maud Gonne and my hope renewed again. If I could go to her and prove by putting my hand in the fire till I had burnt it badly would not that make her understand that devotion like mine should [not] be thrown away lightly. Often as I went to see her I had this thought in mind and I do not think it was fear of pain that prevented me but fear of being mad. I wonder at moments if I was not really mad.

In August 1896 he went with Arthur Symons to stay with Edward Martyn at Tillyra Castle in Galway and while there met Lady Gregory from nearby Coole Park. Yeats wrote to William Sharp: '. . . I invoked one night the spirits of the moon and saw between sleep and waking a beautiful woman firing an arrow among the stars. That night she appeared to Symons who is staying here, and so impressed him that he wrote a poem on her, the only one he ever wrote to a dream, calling her the fountain of all song or some such phrase. . . .'[20] Yeats and Symons then went on to the Aran Islands. Yeats was engaged upon a novel, *The Speckled Bird*, of which only excerpts have been published, which was to have the Aran Islands and Paris as backgrounds. From the Aran Islands they went, in September, to Rosses Point and Sligo. Symons wrote of his experiences in the *Savoy*. It seems probable that Symons accompanied Yeats to Paris in December of the same year. Yeats wrote to O'Leary from the Hôtel Corneille, 5, Rue Corneille, Paris: '. . . I have come here to study some local things and people for a novel which I have contracted with Lawrence & Bullen to write.' (*Letters*, p. 267.) Yeats was also anxious to consult Liddell (Macgregor) Mathers for support in establishing an order of Celtic mysteries on Castle Rock in Lough Key. His state of mind at this time was such, however, that it seems unlikely that he had any very certain notion of what his real objects were. Jeffares writes: 'He was on the verge of dissipation, taking hashish, and within the edge of that state where he could easily have taken permanently to drink. The effect of the MacGregor Matherses upon his depressed introspective, unhinged state was not good. He was brought further from normality, involved in the unreal maze of magical speculation . . .' (p. 109). It appears, in retrospect as though Yeats only narrowly escaped the fate of those others of 'The Tragic Generation' whose ivory towers crumbled from within. That he did so appears to have been due to the patronage and kind nursing of Lady Gregory and to the turbulence of Irish politics. Maud Gonne's continuing participation in the latter no doubt was an incentive to him to re-enter the arena from which, as has been seen, he had never for long been absent.

REFERENCES

1 Jepson, p. 237.
2 Ernest A. Boyd, *Ireland's Literary Renaissance* (Dublin, 1916), p. 189.
3 *The Letters of W. B. Yeats*, pp. 137, 181. Hereinafter, quotations from the letters will be referred to in the text by page number.
4 Boyd, p. 191.
5 Wade, p. 217.
6 A. N. Jeffares, *W. B. Yeats, Man and Poet* (London, 1949), p. 80.
7 Wade, p. 24.
8 *Collected Poems* (London, 1950), p. 524.
9 *Autobiographies*, pp. 254–255.
10 *Autobiographies*, pp. 302–303.
11 Pater, *Selected Works*, Ed. Aldington (London, 1948), p. 233, and again on p. 240.
12 Jeffares, p. 93.
13 The BBC broadcast was printed in the *Listener*, No. 405, 14 October, 1936. It has since been reprinted in *W. B. Yeats, Essays and Introductions* (London, 1961). From the last I have quoted pp. 494–495, 497.
14 Louis MacNeice, *The Poetry of W. B. Yeats* (New York, 1941), p. 63.
15 *Autobiographies*, pp. 309, 318–319.

[16] 'From unpublished material', quoted by A. N. Jeffares in *W. B. Yeats, Man and Poet* (London, 1949), p. 99.

[17] See *The Letters*, p. 260.

[18] *Ibid.*, comment by Wade, p. 195.

[19] Jeffares, p. 105.

[20] *The Letters*, pp. 266–267. Yeats wrote that Symons did not know of his invocation.

CHAPTER V

Arthur Symons

YEATS, writing of the other Rhymers, had described their 'provincialism' as 'curable', his own as 'incurable', as we have seen. To all appearances, Arthur Symons more than any other Rhymer had undergone the 'cure'. When Yeats got to know him during the year at Fountain Court he was completely the cosmopolitan man of letters. But the childhood and youth of Symons had been provincial to the point of torture. His parents were strict Cornish Methodists, and his neighbours and surroundings completely alien to the awakening temperament and already well-established interests of the boy.[1] This environmental antipathy made him take refuge in reading to such an extent that by the age of seventeen he had a prodigious fund of learning. His particular interests then are indicated in his *Study of Walter Pater* (London, 1932), p. 91:

> . . . What Browning was to me in verse, Pater from about the age of seventeen, had been to me in prose. . . . It was from reading Pater's *Studies in the History of the Renaissance*, in its first edition on ribbed paper (I have the feel of it still in my fingers) that I realized that prose also could be a fine art.

His love for and knowledge of Browning was made plain to the literary world when at the age of twenty-one he achieved the publication of *An Introduction to the Study of Browning* (London, 1886). This was no magical stroke of fate. For several years Symons had been struggling to rescue himself from obscure surroundings by turning, in poems and article upon article, to the periodicals, without success. This book was the golden key to the world he desired. Pater, his idol, praised it in the *Guardian*, Meredith had a good word for it and, perhaps above all, Browning wrote to its author a glowing letter thanking him for 'its generosity of appreciation.'[2] His life *began* in 1886. London beckoned, and work as an editor of the Quarto Shakespeare was combined with the writing of further articles, the *National Review* (which paid a pound a page) accepting one on the Provençal poet, Mistral. Ernest Rhys met Symons at the British Museum and offered him, as he had offered Yeats, a book to prepare for the Camelot Series. It was to be an edition of Leigh Hunt's essays. Another association which Symons made about this time was with Havelock Ellis who was editor of the 'Mermaid' series of Jacobean and Restoration dramatists. Symons was a great admirer of these and in 1887 was entrusted with the preparation of the plays of Massinger. In 1888 Symons was working on an annotated edition of *Twelfth Night* for the 'Henry Irving Shakespeare' and trying in vain to correspond with Villiers de l'Isle-Adam, many of whose works were difficult to obtain and of whom he wished to write a critical study. By 1889 he was corresponding with Rémy de Gourmont and seeking his good offices with Villiers de l'Isle-Adam. Symons' article on Villiers de l'Isle-Adam appeared in July of that year. The following year saw the publication of Symons' first book of verse, *Days and Nights*, containing poems written between 1884 and 1888.

Havelock Ellis, who combined the roles of medical doctor and literary editor, decided to take Symons to Paris for his first visit in September 1889. Ellis had lost his editorship of the 'Mermaid' series when the publisher sold out to Unwin. The visit appears to have been a discreet and temperate venture but it created in Symons a passion for further and more exploratory visits. By the Spring of 1890 both men were back again and installed at the Hôtel Corneille, that hotel which Balzac had described and in which Baudelaire had slept.

On this visit Symons had letters of introduction from his London literary acquaintances, many of whom, like Gosse, were socially distinguished. Such letters enabled him, with Ellis, to penetrate the *salons*, where they met Taine and Rodin among others. More important, however, were the café introductions which brought Symons face to face with the Symbolist poets whom he revered. The following extract, from *Colour Studies in Paris* (London, 1918), pp. 41–43, recreates the scene:

> . . . a wheel of memory seems to turn in my head like a kaleidoscope, flashing out the pictures of my own that I keep there. The great sleepy and fiery head of Verlaine is in so many of them. He lies back in his corner at the Café François Premier, with his eyes half shut; he drags on my arm as we go up the boulevard together; he shows me his Bible in the little room up the back

> stairs. . . . I see Mallarmé as he opens the door to me on that fourth floor of the Rue de Rome, with his exquisite manner of welcome. Catulle Mendès lectures on the poetry of the Parnassians, reading Glatigny's verses with his suave and gliding intonation. I see Maeterlinck in all the hurry of a departure, between two portmanteaus; Marcel Schwob in a quiet corner by his own fireside, discussing the first Quarto of *Hamlet*. Maurice Barrès stands before an after-luncheon camera, with the Princess Mathilde on his arm, in an improvised group on the lawn. Jean Moréas with his practical air, thunders out a poem of his own to a waitress in a Bouillon Duval. I find myself by the side of Adolphe Retté at a strange performance in which a play of Tola Dorian is followed by a play of Rachilde. Stuart Merrill introduces me to an editor at the Bullier. Vielé-Griffin speaks English with an evident reluctance at the office of the *Mercure de France*, where Henri de Régnier is silent under his eye-glass. . . .

It is hardly surprising that the comments upon the Rhymers' Club which Symons made were somewhat disparaging and that he should refer to Dowson enjoying 'the real thing' in Paris.

It does not appear that Symons became a very regular frequenter of the Rhymers' Club meetings which began in the year following that stirring Paris visit. He was extremely busy, socially as well as professionally, and one must look for his association with other Rhymers mainly in casual contacts away from the Cheshire Cheese. His friendship with Yeats has been described. It was in March, 1891, that he moved into the rooms in Fountain Court, Temple.[3] The idea of moving there had come from George Moore whom Symons had first met on the Paris visit in 1890. Moore had invited Symons to call on him in London at his rooms in the Temple. Charmed by the place, Symons had watched for an opportunity of moving into similar rooms and taken it when it was offered.

Some understanding of the attitude to life underlying Symons' great activity at this time may be derived from this passage from Pater:

> Life in modern London even, in the heavy glow of summer, is stuff sufficient for the fresh imagination of a youth to build his 'palace of art' of; and the very sense and enjoyment of an experience in which all is new are but enhanced, like that glow of summer itself, by the thought of its brevity, giving him something of a gambler's zest in the apprehension, by dexterous act or diligently appreciative thought, of the highly coloured moments which are to pass away so quickly. [*Marius the Epicurean*, New York, 1935, p. 178.]

A look at a letter of Symons' written from Fountain Court to Ernest Rhys at the beginning of the 'nineties will give an impression of the dominance of this attitude.

Fountain Court
The Temple
Friday March 4th [1892?]
The Day of Judgment

My dear Rhys,

Thanks for your kind letter. I shall let off steam once again by writing to you, as I have so often done before.

'And the evening and the morning were the First Night.' It is now a quarter to 5. After a strange night—which seems to me now like a dream, so wild and whirling was that carnival of fancy dresses, that dancing hubbub—I woke to find, with your letter, a letter from Albert Chevalier (with whom I am to sup at midnight tomorrow) and another from Minnie Cunningham (who is coming to see me 'after the matinée, about 5'). On my way to send a telegram to a lady, offering her a seat for tonight, I find a delightful folio, 1650, 2nd edition of the 'Vulgar Errors,' which I carry home at a cost of 1/6. Then out again, meet my publisher in the street, whom I am going to see; a few minutes after, meet Pierrot of Le Baiser—Bernard Gould: we chat beside the photographer in Burlington Arcade. Then the whim takes me to explore Soho, and I consider old furniture in Wardour Street with the eyes of a millionaire, and wander off into absolutely unknown regions. At last I get back to my Court of the Fountain—to find a letter in marvellous French from my friend M. Peticocu, a Roumanian Impresario, the father of the most wonderful contortionist in the world, saying that he has postponed his departure so that he may accept my invitation to dinner on Sunday, or, as he puts it, 'seulement pour avoir l'honeure de etre d'en votre agreable société (*sic*). And as the gentleman is coming at 5, and I lunch with Raffalovich at 1.45, I pray that a fiery cab horse may be found outside a certain door in Mayfair.

And what shall I do now? Play Berlioz's Marche au Supplice? For the Fates themselves don't know what will happen tonight—now whether one of the contending actresses will get into a cab at the last moment, and leave me minus one of our pieces. That infernal Olga!

[A play of Symons' was to be performed that night. Rhys says that it was a translation of d'Annunzio, but I suspect that this may be incorrect.]

It is 4.30 a.m. and I have just returned from a supper-party—saved, I trust, not damned! Tomorrow and the newspapers!

Well, they are fairly favourable. Here are one or two. I am not satisfied of course, but who ever is?

Yours ever
Arthur Symons

I open this again to tell you of a strange girl I met at the Frankaus' last night—an extraordinary looking young jewess, about 20, with a long lithe body like a snake, a great red dangerous mouth, and enormous dark amber eyes that shut and then expand like great poisonous flowers. 'Nuffing amuses me,' she said, with her curious childish lisp, 'everyfing bores me. Nuffing ever did amuse me. I have nuffing to amuse me, nobody to be amused with. I don't care for men, women's talk always bore me. What am I to do? I don't know what to do with myself. All I care for is to sleep. Tell me what is there that will give me a new sensation?' And she lay back, and gazed at me through her half-shut lids. I bent down and whispered 'Opium.' Her eyes opened with almost a flash of joy. 'Yes, there is opium. Where can I get it? Am I too old to begin?'

I wonder when I shall meet her again.[4]

In April 1891 Symons had set off for Avignon where he met Roumanille, a friend of Mistral who was then engaged elsewhere and had provided the introduction by letter.[5] Then Symons moved on to discover the enchantment of 'the dead city' of Arles (later he was to translate part of d'Annunzio's *La Cittá Morta* there). Thence to Barcelona, Madrid, Burgos, and back *via* Hendaye and Bordeaux to London and to his parents, who were now established at Buckingham, by May.[6] His parents had always been moving since he was a small child, and Arthur Symons seems to have absorbed this nomadic trait. It was constant peregrination, besides his social 'whirl' which must have made him an infrequent visitor to the 'Cheese'. By July of the same year he was off to Berlin.[7] He hated the place. The friends with whom he stayed were sailing from Hamburg for America and he sailed with them to Le Havre. By September he was at St. Leonards in Sussex with a friend.[7]

The following year, 1892, was even busier. He was on the regular staff of the *Athenaeum;* he contributed an article on Verlaine to the new periodical *Black and White*[7]; his second book of poems, *Silhouettes*, was published by Elkin Mathews and John Lane. He was also appointed a critic of the music hall and ballet by the *Star*. The poems in *Silhouettes* are more restrained in tone than those of his first volume: they are 'impressions'—of a sunset, rain, women, dancers, Londoners. It is evident that Symons has read Baudelaire and Verlaine but it is only their superficial characteristics which he captures, while lacking the intensity of emotion and experience which make their work meaningful. For all his choice of exotic themes, 'The Absinthe-Drinker', 'Javanese Dancers', 'Maquillage', he remains outside his subjects, too evidently the young Englishman hankering after forbidden fruit. One of the most successful poems is, perhaps, 'Pastel', where the poet has remained within his limitations and achieved the modest effect which the title implies:

The light of our cigarettes
Went and came in the gloom:
It was dark in the little room.

Dark, and then, in the dark,
Sudden, a flash, a glow,
And a hand and a ring I know.

And then, through the dark, a flush
Ruddy and vague, the grace
(A rose!) of her lyric face.[8]

Professor Lhombreaud remarks upon the probable influence of Verlaine's poem, 'Femme et Chatte', in which, instead of glowing cigarettes there are the phosphorescent points of light from the eyes of both cat and woman. By quoting Verlaine's poem in full here I think I may illustrate that the influence has not been a very profound one (not that Professor Lhombreaud suggests that it has, of course):

Elle jouait avec sa chatte;
Et c'était merveille de voir
La main blanche et la blanche patte
S'ébattre dans l'ombre du soir.

Elle cachait—la scélérate!—
Sous ces mitaines de fil noir
Ses meurtriers ongles d'agate,
Coupants et clairs comme un rasoir.

L'autre aussi faisait la sucrée
Et rentrait sa griffe acérée,
Mais le diable n'y perdait rien . . .

Et dans le boudoir où, sonore,
Tintait son rire aérien,
Brillaient quatre points de phosphore.

In Verlaine's poem we are in the presence of two creatures whose shared feline characteristics are the point of the comparison. Symons' 'flush, ruddy and vague,' and the palpitant excitement of his rhythm, are a long way from the leisured, dispassionate appraisal which the Frenchman makes. Cats do not flush, and it is on the woman's 'claws' rather than her 'ring' that his gaze hovers. Symons' poem at once recalls Browning to me; not only is the mood a pure, lyrical mood (with nothing 'Decadent' about it) such as that of 'Meeting at Night', but also the technique, with its dramatically broken rhythm and staccato monosyllables, its parenthetic exclamation, is plainly learnt from the nineteenth-century master of the dramatic lyric.

In May 1892, Symons, in his role of ballet critic, went to Paris to see the artistry of Aristide Bruant and La Mélinite and the dancers of the Moulin Rouge.[9] Next month an article of his on Verlaine appeared in the *National Review*. It began:

> The art of Paul Verlaine is something new, absolutely new, to poetry. *Romances sans paroles*—songs without words—is the name of one of his volumes, and his poetry at its best might almost be called disembodied song. It is an art of impressionism—sometimes as delicate, as pastoral, as Watteau, sometimes as sensitively modern as Whistler, sometimes as brutally modern as Degas.[10]

Back in London in July, Symons entertained John Addington Symonds, with whom he had been in correspondence for some time:

> . . . Dowson turned up, then the ballet-girls, one after another, whose laughter and whose youth always enchanted me; then Symonds, whose entrance seemed to disturb them; they began to be curiously nervous, and he by being for a few minutes nervously shy. Yet when, with the gravity of a Doge, he handed round the tea and I the cakes and cigarettes, we suddenly became quite at home. Later on we tried the effect of haschisch—that slow intoxication, that elaborate experiment in visionary sensations . . .[11]

Jepson wrote of Symons:

> Indeed I think that among the English poets he was the happiest exponent of the decadent formula. But in our ignorance we did not take him so seriously as he was taken in later days.
>
> Touching that decadence, when in the 'nineties we talked of the decadent poets we did not mean exactly what the journalists of today [1933] mean when they write with shocked pens of the decadent poets of the 'nineties. We were speaking of a French school of poets, of whom Verlaine was the chief, in whose verse there was a certain fall, a *décadence*, which you find in the best verse of Mr. Arthur Symons and in some of the poems of Ernest Dowson. It may be that the journalists have not heard of the French decadents, and having been misled by the word, their

mistake was quite natural, for, oddly enough, it never struck me when I was with those poets that I was in the decadent atmosphere of the later Roman Empire.

I have known Beardsley rather noisy at dinner, but hardly in a decadent way, and you could not call the gusto with which he ate the meal decadent; again it was not really the right epithet to apply to the appetite with which Dowson would fall upon a *Wiener Schnitzel*. Un-English, if you like—I mean that all of them preferred a sole Montmorenci at the Café Royal to boiled mutton and caper sauce at Wilkinson's—but not decadent: no. And hang it all! they all on occasion wore top hats.

To put it exactly: Dowson was as decadent in the journalistic or later Roman sense as Keats.

You might perhaps call Wilde decadent, if you liked; but after all inversion, and I am inclined rather to consider him a convert, does not certainly imply decadence. At least there must have been some stout fellows in the Theban band. And what was he decadent from? Tom Moore or Charles Lever?

But perhaps I am wrong and there was decadence: a fall from Lewis Morris's *Epic of Hades*, say, to the sonnet *To One in Bedlam*, and from Frith's *Derby Day* to the illustrations of Mr. Smith's translation of the *Lysistrata*.[12]

I have quoted this more for its humorous and anecdotal value than for any light it may shed on the vexed word 'Decadent'. Did the word 'Decadent' only mean the style in which verse was written? Is an examination of eating habits a sure way of ascertaining spiritual health? Does Jepson imagine that the 'later Romans' were delicate in their manners on the couch? Does the comparison with Keats put 'exactly' what he had in common with Dowson?

Richard Le Gallienne, as we have seen, attacked 'Decadence' as early as 1892. What did *he* understand by it?

Literary decadence consists in the euphuistic expression of isolated observations. To notice only the picturesque effects of a beggar's rags as Gautier; the colour-scheme of a tippler's nose, like M. Huysmans; to consider one's mother merely prismatically, like Mr. Whistler—these are examples of the decadent attitude. At the bottom, decadence is merely limited thinking, often insane thinking. . . .[13]

When Arthur Symons, finding this to be a travesty of his own idea of decadence, replied by an article in November, 1893, it was not in terms calculated to soothe Le Gallienne. Symons wrote of

. . . the qualities that we find in the Greek, the Latin, decadence: an intense self-consciousness, a restless curiosity in research, an

> over-subtilizing refinement upon refinement, a spiritual and moral perversity. If what we call the classic is indeed the supreme art —those qualities of perfect simplicity, perfect sanity, perfect proportion, the supreme qualities—then this representative literature of to-day, interesting, beautiful, novel as it is, is really a new and beautiful and interesting disease. . . .[14]

Symons' description is, to me, almost a just one. The issue is not here a literary one at all—it is a moral one—and this it is that has bedevilled the use of the word 'Decadent' right up to the present day. Le Gallienne belonged to the school of those who have moral preconceptions of what art *ought* to be like. Therefore he and the hearty John-Bull-type writers of the period from 1880 to the present day are incomplete artists. They imagine that the sanity, balance, and harmony of the ancient world may be attained by pretending that we have those qualities. Symons did not shrink from a full awareness of the true spiritual condition of *fin-de-siècle* Europe: his poetry, or more particularly the poetry of the French Symbolists for whom he was an invaluable intermediary, expresses the cultural and spiritual breakdown of the time. The old values which were based on Christianity had waned with the weakening of faith; the humanistic culture which, in such an age as the Elizabethan, expressed the soul of a people, had been perverted and degraded by a commercially governed popular press; the poets had either been absorbed by the commercial or ideological struggle or had retreated to ivory towers of subjectivism. Nor is there anything necessarily reprehensible about an ivory tower. In the Dark Ages monks remained fast within their monasteries and the light of knowledge was kept burning. As they became increasingly aware of the modern dilemma to which I have referred, and which is still ours today, many poets withdrew from a world becoming meaningless and sought in myth and symbol to establish correspondence between the phenomena of that world which seemed, as Yeats remarked, 'a bundle of fragments'.

One may attempt an historical definition of the Decadent Movement as one which is permeated by an awareness of a cultural and spiritual decline in modern Europe and which expresses this in its impact upon personalities. The expression may take many forms. Symons has summarized some of them above but I think goes too far in describing the literature itself as a disease. A clinician who writes a report on psychic or physiological disturbance is not himself diseased. The Decadent poets are trying to come to terms with the disease within society, or to escape from it, and, though we may not always approve of their methods, their awareness of social dissolution is morally on a higher plane than the pretence which a materialist society makes that it is whole and sane. Thus another characteristic of the Decadents is their attempt to shock a complacent society into an awareness of its weakness. Owen Seaman was providing a support for, rather than an attack upon, the Decadents when he wrote:

> *The erotic affairs that you fiddle aloud*
> *Are as vulgar as coin of the mint;*
> *And you merely distinguish yourself from the crowd*
> *By the fact that you put 'em in print.*[15]

The implication is that there is a large part of everyday life which is too shameful to be described: hardly, I think, a 'healthier' attitude.

Finally, much confusion exists in criticism concerning this period through the misinterpretation of the word 'Decadent' as a term of abuse, a reflection upon the personal life of the writer concerned. It cannot be too strongly emphasized that the word, as far as literature is concerned, refers to a type of work and not a type of person. A case can be made that many whose work was of the Decadent School led somewhat depraved lives. It will be found, however, that an equally strong case of this kind can be made against writers of all schools of thought, not to mention men in quite other walks of life. But, as Seaman says, they don't put their affairs 'in print'.

Having defended the right of the Decadent Movement to an honourable place in literature, I must add that those English poets to whom I have referred as imitators of the French Symbolists and Decadents, and I am thinking particularly of Symons and Dowson, differed considerably from their models, as nearly all imitators do. The difference has been clearly expressed by Mr. Wendell Harris in an article 'Innocent Decadence: The Poetry of the *Savoy*'. He wrote, concerning some of the Decadent contributions to the *Savoy:*

> It seems clear that the 'decadence' of these poems must be carefully distinguished from that of French poets such as Baudelaire, Verlaine, and Rimbaud. The similarity resides in the aura of disillusionment which envelops the poetry of both groups, but among such poets of the 1890s as Dowson and Symons we find little celebration of a perverse and violent search for new experiences, few complaints of true ennui, little remorse for sins of the past. The English melancholy flowered essentially from a sense that love, beauty, and ideality flaunt themselves ever just out of reach. The 'ideal' love or the 'perfect' woman who briefly touches the poet's life or achieves existence in his imagination, and thus renders him henceforth necessarily unsatisfied, becomes a symbol of the ideal for him. It is true that

there is an unhealthiness in that mentality which, having envisioned the unqualifiedly good and beautiful, ever afterward is plunged in despair at imperfect reality, but this is not the antic, twistedly analytic despair associated with the French *décadents.*[16]

(I must disagree, however, concerning the 'unhealthiness' of despair at imperfect reality: we are not, after all, concerned with 'mentalities' but with poems, and it is permitted to poets to express man's discontent with the earthbound.)

In November, 1893 Verlaine came to London at Symons' invitation and gave a lecture there and at Oxford. He slept in the rooms at Fountain Court which Yeats was later to occupy for a while and which actually belonged to Havelock Ellis. To Verlaine's lecture on 'Contemporary French Poetry', in the hall of Barnard's Inn, Holborn, the Rhymers came in a body.

Katherine Bradley and Edith Cooper (who wrote as 'Michael Field') were present and gave this account of Verlaine in *Works and Days* (London, 1933):

> 22 November, 1893. Verlaine reads his own poems at Barnard's Inn—a most 'seizing' occasion (in the French sense). The picturesque hall—eighty to a hundred intellectual listeners, many of them women—the personality of the reader, that can be summarized by Strafford's 'thorough' (for Verlaine is as extreme a devotee as he is extreme a sinner): the June-rose beauty of his young neophyte Symons; the low melodies of that cracked instrument his voice, and the congruity between the poems and the poet—all those things made the time from a quarter to nine until ten almost singularly new.
>
> When Verlaine and Symons came in, the obvious simile was that of a rose bush beside a blasted thorn; Symons almost supported his lame companion to the chair and then retired to the second side row. . . . [p. 188.]
>
> . . . he was very, *very* judicious in the choice of his poems, and there was not a trace of 'vine-leaves in his hair'—I was going to write, but I must rather say round his beautiful, bald skull. It was such an English scene—Satan in a frock-coat, reading religious poetry and darting pitch-spark glances at a company incapable of understanding the tragedies of hell (even the devils believe and tremble), still less its bouts of free revel.[17]

The Rhymers accompanied him after the lecture to the Crown Public House, a rendezvous which I mentioned in an earlier chapter and of which a description may not now come amiss. It was 'a very ordinary public-house of the richer kind':

> At its north-eastern corner was its saloon bar, and in that bar after eleven o'clock and until half-past twelve, closing time, one would find poets and painters, dramatists and ballet girls (of the more serious kind), critics and patrons, novelists and hangers-on of the arts.
>
> Do not think it was an ordinary saloon bar. One entered, and the narrow space opened out and disclosed a bar-parlour. The bar itself flanked one of its sides. Prosperous cab-proprietors and bookmakers' runners and the male assistants at the neighbouring music-halls and theatres stood at that bar and drank. The patrons of whom I treat had nothing to do with them. My friends were of the *intelligentzia;* they talked learnedly about the ballet and Walter Sickert and the latest art movement in France and Edmund Gosse's last insincerity. There were settees round the wall and we sat on them and drank hot gin and water. Certain celebrities you were quite sure of finding. Selwyn Image was one of them and Herbert Horne another, and with Herbert Horne would be Arthur Symons. These last you could depend upon to turn up within a few minutes of the closing of the Empire and the Alhambra. . . . Ernest Dowson would, as likely as not, be first to arrive. These were the regulars. . . .
>
> . . . The occasional frequenters one could number by the score. Hubert Crackanthorpe, Rothenstein [Will], Beardsley, Oscar—but not very often—Robert Ross, Percy Addleshaw, Lionel Johnson, John Lane (observant and not at all in his element), John Gray, Conder, Stewart Headlam, Victor Plarr, Max Beerbohm, Kaines Jackson, Theodore Wratislaw. They did not all drink gin—and, to the best of my memory, with one exception, no one of them ever got drunk. The visit to The Crown was not a dissipation; it was the end of the day's work, a chance of meeting and talking with congenial friends, of exchanging ideas. It was far better, if less comfortable, than the Café Royal which succeeded it, for its limited space made it necessary that much of the conversation should be general. . . .
>
> . . . Symons brought Verlaine along to The Crown and, with Verlaine, Edmund Gosse, who had been in the Chair at Barnard's Inn and who looked extremely unhappy at finding himself at such an hour in the bar-parlour of a London public-house.[18]

Verlaine remained in London for a short time. Dowson was anxious to have closer contact with him than he had enjoyed at the meeting and at The Crown. He wrote to Victor Plarr about this and about the verses which he was submitting for the *Second Book of the Rhymers' Club*, then in preparation:

Bridge Dock,
Limehouse.

Cher Vieux,

Do you like the enclosed verses enough to include them in the Book in lieu of 'Benedictio Domini'? Johnson to whom I conveyed the weighty packet seems to like them the best of my budget. He was very amicable and we drank much absinthe together. I voted for 6 of your poems with much difficulty for I liked them all so much that I wished to see them all included. I placed the 'Cinerarium', 'Breton Beggar', and 'Nejnun' first—of L's I think I most admired the Cavalier and Mystic. Verlaine is after all still in London. I am dining with Horne and Horne Père at the Constitutional tonight to meet him. So that if I have the courage I will even suggest to the Master that he should honour his disciples with a visit to the Cheese. A bientôt—with all amenities to Mesdames Votre Mère et votre femme et à cette chère Bébé.

T. à toi

ERNEST DOWSON[19]

After the appearance of the *Second Book of the Rhymers' Club* in the Spring of 1894 the Rhymers appear to have met less frequently and gradually to have separated. From a study of the Mathews papers at the University of Reading, Professor Karl Beckson (*op. cit.* p. 10) notes that Elkin Mathews wrote to Herbert Horne on 20 September, 1894 concerning a Third Book of the Rhymers' Club and whether he, Mathews, or Lane was to be the publisher. Also noted is an undated letter from Ernest Radford to G. A. Greene urging the choice of Mathews.

A postcard, postmarked 13 May, 1895, from Greene to Mathews, tells of a Rhymers' Club dinner postponed until June and invites Mathews to attend with a guest. From the G. C. R. Greene Collection, Professor Beckson notes a postcard from Yeats to G. A. Greene dated 2 November, 1896 convening a meeting of Rhymers for 'Wednesday at 5 p.m.' Beckson comments that Yeats may have been attempting to resuscitate a club which had long since died.

Most of the Rhymers had formed their own circles of friends and a new form of collective publication was offered in the forthcoming *Yellow Book*. In April the first number of this quarterly appeared from the publishing house of Elkin Mathews and John Lane. (From the third volume it was published by John Lane alone.) An extract from a review of the first number in the *Athenaeum* will be found on page 151. A number of the Rhymers contributed to the series of thirteen volumes from 1894 to 1897, including John Davidson, Dowson, Le Gallienne, Yeats and Symons.

Symons contributed to the shocking-power of the first volume with his poem 'Stella Maris' in which he dared to describe physical love. One stanza will, I think, suffice of this poem which is in no other way remarkable:

O lost and wrecked, how long ago,
Out of the drowning past, I know
You come to call me, come to claim
My share of your delicious shame.
Child, I remember, and can tell
One night we loved each other well,
And one night's love, at least or most
Is not so small a thing to boast.
You were adorable, and I
Adored you to infinity,
That nuptial night too briefly borne
To the oblivion of morn.
Ah! no oblivion, for I feel
Your lips deliriously steal
Along my neck, and fasten there;
I feel the perfume of your hair,
I feel your breast that heaves and dips
Desiring my desirous lips,
And that ineffable delight
When souls turn bodies, and unite
In the intolerable, the whole
Rapture of the embodied soul.

[*Poems*, I, 111]

The trial of Oscar Wilde began in 1895 while the fifth volume of the *Yellow Book* was in preparation. It led to the publisher Lane's break with the Decadents for representations were made to Henry Harland, the editor, by William Watson (persuaded by Mrs. Humphrey Ward and Alice Meynell) against the continued inclusion of Beardsley's drawings. The frightened editor and publisher yielded, and excluded Beardsley's drawings without consulting him, so that he resigned. From then the *Yellow Book* lost its Decadent aura. It had from the start included authors who were in no sense Decadent and the number of these came to predominate.

About the same time in 1895 that Yeats was attempting to console himself in the company of 'Diana Vernon' for Maud Gonne's refusal, Symons was tormented by love for a ballet dancer whom he had first seen on stage at the Empire. He had known her for over a year and in August, 1895, he had a final scene with her and left in despair for Dieppe.[20] The effect of this disappointment upon his verse was similar in kind to that of Yeats's troubles upon his—a dilettantism of the emotions gives way to a harder personal note. The result, in Symons' case, became apparent when the poems of this year appeared as *Amoris Victima* in September 1896. The collection of his verse published in 1895, however, *London Nights*, is the fruit of his year of frequenting the ballet and music halls and is the most Decadent of his works. Both John Lane and Heinemann refused it, as they perhaps would not have done but for the Wilde trial, and it was left to Leonard Smithers to show the necessary courage. The volume included the poem 'Stella Maris'. Principally it consists of delicate pastel poems conjuring the strange beauty of gas-lit foggy streets, and the wings of theatres and music-halls where the seemingly ugly, realistic side of life is seen in poignant juxtaposition with the art into which it may be transmuted. The affinity with the painters Degas and Toulouse-Lautrec is evident in such themes and, of course, Verlaine had already discovered the London which, with its grotesque contrasts and mysterious veils of grey light, he would appear to have established in the minds of Frenchmen as their image of English metropolitan life. Where better than in London may the 'nuance' be seen:

> *Car nous voulons la Nuance encor,*
> *Pas la Couleur, rien que la nuance!*
> ['Art Poétique']

One may note that it is the glamorous aspects of city life which principally inspire Symons. He seldom attempts, as Davidson did, to transmute the commonplace into poetry.

In October, 1895, Symons was still in Dieppe.[21] This had become the favourite across-channel rendezvous of painters such as Sickert and Rothenstein who were there on this occasion, as also was Conder. Dowson had been staying there since June in a small hotel near the Cathedral and Beardsley had arrived in September. With these men as a nucleus, Leonard Smithers, solicitor and publisher of under-the-counter 'literature', as also of fine books, proposed the launching of a new periodical to supply the place of the renegade *Yellow Book*, now become all too patently a 'house' magazine of John Lane. The first number of this periodical, *The Savoy*, appeared in January 1896. It began as a quarterly and continued so until the July number, after which it appeared monthly. It was not well received owing to almost 'national' hostility to the Decadents which the trial of Wilde had brought to a head. W. H. Smith, the bookselling chain, refused to circulate it and its last number appeared in December. This, number 8, was composed entirely by Arthur Symons and Aubrey Beardsley. Among the contributors to the eight numbers had been: Beardsley, Mathilde Blind, Conrad, Crackanthorpe, Dowson, Havelock Ellis, Gosse, Image, Lionel Johnson, Cesare Lombroso, 'Fiona MacLeod', Mallarmé, Moréas,

George Moore, Sarojini Naidu (an Indian girl), O'Sullivan, Verhaéren, Verlaine, Wratislaw and Yeats. Artist contributors included Max Beerbohm, J. E. Blanche, Conder, Phil May, Will Rothenstein, Shannon and Sickert. One wonders if ever again will be seen such an array of talent and genius between the covers of a magazine on a bookstall. It cost two shillings.

Symons' journey with Yeats, in 1896, to Ireland and the Aran Islands has already been mentioned. Both were suffering from disappointments in love affairs and from the artistic *impasse* which seemed, in each case differently, to have been reached. To Symons the failure of the *Savoy* represented the futility of trying to combat the increasingly Philistine and Imperialistic spirit of the times. In Paris, in December, he wrote 'Perfect Grief' in which he considers the woman whom he loved as dead. By New Year's Eve he was in Rome where he met again Count Florimont de Basterot whom he had been with in Ireland.[22] He met also Count Giuseppe Primoli, a friend of d'Annunzio, and the Comtesse de la Tour who had invited him to her *salon* on the Via Giulia. She became a useful friend to him. His mind still dwelt upon his lost love in his *Roman Elegies*. From Rome he went on to Naples and found its stridency antipathetic. He was weary but urged on to restless wanderings which in 1897 and 1898 took him to Venice, Moscow, Bayreuth, Warsaw, St Petersburg, Prague, Budapest, the Rhine Valley, Auvergne, Provence and Spain, to mention some of the places. Concerning Symons' literary standing, Professor Lhombreaud wrote:

> [In the years 1889 to 1898, he] . . . had been progressively recognized in his capacity as a critic; but at the end of the century his reputation hardly reached beyond a narrow circle of friends and a restricted literary public. It was for his qualities as an artist and polished prose-writer that he was known and appreciated, rather than for his manifestoes of Art for Art's Sake, or even for the majority of the poems in his first three books.[22]

While at Auvergne in 1898 with the Comtesse de la Tour he began one of his most difficult undertakings so far, his book *The Symbolist Movement in Literature* (originally to have been entitled the *Decadent Movement in Literature*) which appeared in 1900. This book is regarded by most commentators on Symons as a kind of peak achievement never really surpassed, and I agree with this view. Professor Lhombreaud quotes, in contradiction of this view, from Symons:

> The book is intended to form a part of a series, on which I have been engaged for many years. I am gradually working my

> way towards a concrete expression of a theory, or system of aesthetics, of all the arts. In my book on 'The Symbolist Movement in Literature' I made a first attempt to deal in this way with literature; other volumes, now in preparation, are to follow. [*Plays, Acting and Music*, London, 1903; Lhombreaud, p. 168.]

The other volumes were: *Plays, Acting and Music* (London, 1903), *Studies in Seven Arts* (London, 1906) and *Cities, Sea-coasts and Islands* (London, 1917).

In his dedication of *The Symbolist Movement in Literature*, which is to W. B. Yeats, we can see how an affinity with the mystical bent of that poet had developed through the author's studies in Symbolism:

> I speak often in this book of Mysticism, and that I, of all people, should venture to speak, not quite as an outsider, of such things, will probably be a surprise to many. It will be no surprise to you, for you have seen me gradually finding my way, uncertainly, but inevitably, in that direction which has always been to you your natural direction.[23]

Arthur Symons' summaries, in this book, of eight French poets and their work, make a kind of anthology of Symbolism which is more helpful than much generalization. It is apparent that he has changed his definition of Decadence from the one which he gave in 1893, and which I have quoted. In *The Symbolist Movement* he treats it as principally a question of style, as Jepson did. In the earlier definition, Symons referred to 'a spiritual and moral perversity' as characteristic of 'the Greek, the Latin, decadence', but in *The Symbolist Movement* he wrote:

> . . . As a matter of fact, the term is in its place only when applied to style; to that ingenious deformation of the language, in Mallarmé, for instance, which can be compared with what we are accustomed to call the Greek and Latin of the Decadence. No doubt perversity of form and perversity of matter are often found together, and, among the lesser men especially, experiment was carried far, not only in the direction of style. But a movement which in this sense might be called Decadent could but have been a straying aside from the main road of literature. Nothing, not even conventional virtue, is so provincial as conventional vice; and the desire to 'bewilder the middle-classes' is itself middle-class. The interlude, half a mock-interlude, of Decadence, diverted the attention of the critics while something more serious was in preparation. That something more serious has crystallized, for the time, under the form of Symbolism, in which art returns to the one pathway, leading through beautiful things to the eternal beauty. [p. 4]

Symons, one may infer, has 'put away childish things', and *The Symbolist Movement* is a conspectus of the types of poetic attitude—all having the 'eternal beauty' as their principal focus—which he has come to find most meaningful. It is not an analytical criticism of the Symbolists' poetry that Symons offers the reader, but rather the statement of a creed, copiously illustrated (for so short a work) with biographical detail whose necessity he would, I feel sure, have explained by the inseparability of the lives of these poets from their works. His first chapter, on Gérard de Nerval, contains much which I view as a projection of Symons:

> Like so many dreamers of illimitable dreams, it was the fate of Gérard to incarnate his ideal in the person of an actress. [p. 11]

The result was as unfortunate for Gérard as for Symons. In retrospect, Symons' comment on madness is prophetic of the way he himself was to go within seven years of writing it:

> . . . we owe to the fortunate accident of madness one of the foundations of what may be called the practical aesthetics of Symbolism. [p. 19.]

Symons, recovering from madness, wrote his *Confessions* just as Nerval had written the story of his madness, in *Le Rêve et La Vie*. It is not going too far, I think, to say that during his madness Symons repeatedly identified himself with Nerval, and the *Confessions* reveal the extent to which his forerunner, as it were, had obsessed him.

Symons introduces his book by citing Carlyle's reference to the Symbol: 'In the Symbol proper, what we can call a Symbol, there is ever, more or less distinctly and directly, some embodiment and revelation of the Infinite; the Infinite is made to blend itself with the Finite, to stand visible, and as it were, attainable there.' (p. 2) Symons asserts that, while Symbolism has always been present in literature, the form of Symbolism developed in nineteenth-century France after Nerval is different in that it has become conscious of itself. Just as Yeats believed in 1899 that the arts were about to take on a priestly role, so was the belief in the 'religious' nature of literature shared by Gérard de Nerval, Villiers de l'Isle-Adam, Rimbaud, Verlaine, Laforgue, Mallarmé, Huysmans and Maeterlinck, the discussion of whom makes up this book. Their task has been to free literature from 'exteriority', from rhetoric, from the materialistic tradition in general in order to arrive at a language of the spirit whose object is not definition but the carrying of the spirit beyond the veil of the apparently real to a mystical consciousness of the greater reality of dream and of the consciousness itself:

> Know, once for all, that there is for thee no other universe than that conception thereof which is reflected at the bottom of thy thoughts. [p. 23]

Thus wrote Villiers de l'Isle-Adam, from whom Symons here quotes.

Symons differs from this poet with regard to the lodgement of the highest faculties only in the god-like few. The mind of de l'Isle-Adam was, he comments, 'too abstract to contain pity.' He continues, '. . . he does not realize, as the great novelists realized, that stupidity can be pathetic [in the literal sense], and that there is not a peasant, nor even a self-satisfied bourgeois, in whom the soul has not its part, in whose existence it is not possible to be interested.' (pp. 29–30)

The hunger for the supernatural made Rimbaud also 'a small, narrow, hard, precipitate nature, which had the will to live, and nothing but the will to live; and his verses, and his follies, and his wanderings, and his traffickings were but the breathing of different hours in his day.' (pp. 36–37)

Symons' chapter on Laforgue introduced that poet's work to T. S. Eliot. Symons wrote of Laforgue:

> He has invented a new manner of being René or Werther: an inflexible politeness towards man, woman, and destiny. He composes love-poems hat in hand, and smiles with an exasperating tolerance before all the transformations of the eternal feminine. He is very conscious of death, but his *blague* of death is, above all things, gentlemanly. He will not permit himself, at any moment, the luxury of dropping the mask: not at any moment. [pp. 60–61.]

And thus we have 'J. Alfred Prufrock' and perhaps even T. S. Eliot himself.

The chapter, 'The Later Huysmans', may be seen as an illustration of the kind of thinking which had come to take the place with Symons, as with Huysmans, of the earlier quest for 'impressions'. I shall first quote from the article on Huysmans, (the *earlier* Huysmans) which was collected into *Studies in Prose and Verse* (London, 1904), but omitted from the second edition:

> Des Esseintes is the symbol of all those who have tried to shut themselves in from the natural world, upon an artificial beauty which has no root there. Worshipping colour, sound, perfume, for their own sakes, and for for their ministrations to a more divine beauty, he stupefies himself on the threshold of ecstasy.

And Huysmans, we can scarcely doubt, has passed through the particular kind of haschisch dream which the experience really is. He has realized that the great choice, the choice between the world and something which is not visible in the world, but out of which the visible world has been made, does not lie in the mere contrast of the subtler and grosser senses. He has come to realize what the choice really is, and he has chosen. Yet perhaps the choice is not quite so narrow as Barbey d'Aurévilly thought; perhaps it is a choice between actualizing this dream or actualizing that dream. . . .

. . . And the making of one's life into art is after all the first duty and privilege of every man. It is to escape from material reality into whatever form of ecstasy is our form of spiritual existence. There is the choice; and our happiness, our 'success in life', will depend on our choosing rightly, each for himself, among the forms in which the choice will come to us.[24]

In the chapter 'The Later Huysmans', Symons quotes in translation a passage from Huysman's *Là-Bas*, which indicates that Huysmans was not permanently satisfied with the position depicted in the foregoing:

. . . it is essential to preserve the veracity of the document [the 'colour-scheme of a tippler's nose,' for example?], the precision of detail, the fibrous and nervous language of Realism, but it is equally essential to become the well-digger of the soul, and not to attempt to explain what is mysterious by mental maladies . . .

. . . It is essential, in a word, to follow the great road so deeply dug out by Zola, but it is necessary also to trace a parallel pathway in the air, and to grapple with the within and the after, to create, in a word, a spiritual Naturalism. [p. 76.]

Further on in the same chapter (p. 80), Symons writes:

For in *La Cathédrale* Huysmans does but carry further the principle which he had perceived in *En Route*, showing, as he does, how inert matter, the art of stones, the growth of plants, the unconscious life of beasts, may be brought under the same law of the soul, may obtain, through symbol, a spiritual existence.

And later on the same page:

What is Symbolism if not an establishing of the links which hold the world together, the affirmation of an eternal, minute, intricate, almost invisible life, which runs through the whole universe?

Huysmans' conversion to Roman Catholicism is comparable with those of several others of the writers of the 'nineties. In its liturgy and its cathedrals such as Chartres—the subject of Huysmans' book—is evidence, for some, of *correspondances*, in the Baudelairean sense, within the visible world and between the visible world and the invisible. The development in Huysmans corresponds in many ways to that which takes place in the work of Walter Pater, from the *Renaissance* to *Marius the Epicurean.* I shall refer again to Pater in my closing chapter.

Concerning *The Symbolist Movement in Literature*, T. S. Eliot wrote:

> I myself owe Mr. Symons a great debt: but for having read his book, I should not, in the year 1908, have heard of Laforgue or Rimbaud; I should probably not have begun to read Verlaine; and but for reading Verlaine, I should not have heard of Corbière. So the Symons book is one of those which have affected the course of my life.[25]

In January, 1901, Symons married Rhoda Bowser and, after a few years of happiness, ran into financial worries exacerbated by the cessation of the demand for a sensitive, polite journalism. So greatly was his life disturbed that in 1908 his mind gave way and he was certified insane.[26] Whether the more advanced psychiatry of today would have agreed with the diagnosis or found him manic-depressively psychotic is a question which I am not, of course, qualified to discuss. One is happy not to have to end this chapter on that note, for he made a recovery by about 1910 and slowly returned to a routine of work,[27] even appearing in the Café Royal in the late 1930s.

REFERENCES

[1] Most of the biographical facts in this chapter are from Roger Lhombreaud's *Arthur Symons, A Critical Biography* (London, 1963), hereafter referred to as Lhombreaud.

[2] Lhombreaud, pp. 37, 41, 46, 61.

[3] Lhombreaud, p. 77.

[4] Ernest Rhys, *Letters from Limbo*, pp. 198–201.

[5] Lhombreaud, p. 78.

[6] Lhombreaud, pp. 80, 83, 79.

[7] Lhombreaud, pp. 80, 83, 79.

[8] Arthur Symons, *Poems* (London, 1919), p. 21.

[9] Lhombreaud, p. 90.

[10] *National Review*, June, 1892, p. 501.

[11] From 'A Study of John Addington Symonds' in the *Fortnightly Review*, February 1924, pp. 228–239. Quoted by Lhombreaud, p. 93.

[12] Jepson, *Memories of a Victorian*, p. 215.

[13] *Retrospective Reviews: A Library Log* (London, 1896), I, pp. 24–26. The original article was a review of Churton Collins' *Illustrations of Tennyson*, January, 1892.

[14] *Harper's Monthly Magazine*, November 1893, p. 858.

[15] Quoted from *Punch* by J. Lewis May, *John Lane and the Nineties* (London, 1936), p. 145.

[16] *PMLA*, LXXVII (1962), 629–636.

[17] For the reference to *Works & Days* I am indebted to Ruth Z. Temple, *The Critic's Alchemy* (New York, 1953).

[18] Grant Richards, *Memoirs of a Misspent Youth* (New York, 1933), pp. 338–340.

[19] Longaker, p. 104.

[20] Lhombreaud, p. 119.

[21] Lhombreaud, pp. 121–122.

[22] Lhombreaud, pp. 138, 153, 168.

[23] Arthur Symons, *The Symbolist Movement in Literature* (London): the first edition was imprinted 1899 but, in fact, appeared in 1900. In this study all references to this work are to the Dutton 'Everyman' Series Edition, ed. Richard Ellmann (New York, 1958). Page xx is referred to above.

[24] *Studies in Prose and Verse* (London, 1904), p. 289.

[25] *The Criterion*, January, 1930, p. 357.

[26] Lhombreaud, pp. 185, 247, 269.

[27] Lhombreaud, pp. 185, 247, 269.

CHAPTER VI

The Dowson Legend

IN the August 1896 number of *The Savoy* appeared an article by Arthur Symons (the editor) entitled 'A Literary Causerie: On a Book of Verses'. Though the writer of the verses concerned was not named, there could have been little doubt in the minds of those who knew Ernest Dowson that he was the subject of this biographical sketch. I have reproduced the article on pp. 153–155. Symons' main theme is the contrast between the poetry and the man and he plunges into a lurid depiction of the latter's *nostalgie de boue*, his dissipations and the sorriness of his predicament, with all the enthusiasm and heartlessness of one to whom the artistic presentation of the Decadence which his friend seems to him to ideally typify is more important than that reticence, or even exactitude, which most men would have felt to be an essential ingredient of friendship. In the history of our literature I can call to mind no other such account by a poet of another who is his friend. 'He will not mind, I know, if I speak of him with some of that frankness which we reserve usually for the dead.' Dowson, already afflicted with pthisis, had six years to live. (Not, of course, that Symons could have known that, but Dowson was all too obviously ailing and a victim of 'the suicidal energy of genius'.) Two years earlier both of Dowson's parents had died: his father from an overdose of chloral, his mother—six months after her husband—by self-strangulation. Now Dowson is gently informed that he has: 'an appearance generally somewhat dilapidated, . . . a nature which I can only compare to a weedy garden, its grass trodden down by many feet, but with one small, carefully-tended flower-bed, luminous with lilies.'

The first question to be answered is, is this a true picture of the poet? My answer, which I shall endeavour to support here, is that it is as true as any impressionistic portrait can be. If we look at the portrait of Dowson by Will Rothenstein (opposite p. 62 in Longaker) or at the photograph of Dowson at Oxford, in which he is smartly dressed (opposite p. 32), or at the drawing by Conder (opposite p. 24), the expression 'somewhat dilapidated' seems somehow warranted. The reference to hashish is, however, misleading. It seems, at first sight, extraordinary that Symons should have made it. The occasion mentioned (which is the one depicted in my preceding chapter, p. 63) was, as is here admitted, the fruit of Symons' own sensation-seeking mind, and, writing of that occasion in 1924, Symons did not at all assert that the 'experiment' was disappointing or ludicrous. He wrote of 'that slow intoxication, that elaborate experiment in visionary sensations'.[1] Moreover, Symons elsewhere admits that he himself '. . . took hashish fairly frequently in Fountain Court and in Paris; and the sensations it gave me were wonderful.'[2] In fact, the statement about Dowson, made late in his life and after a long mental illness, were probably exaggerated. The reasonable conclusion seems that Dowson took no more hashish than his associates, including Yeats, did. As to Oxford, we have the word of W. R. Thomas that the hashish-taking there was no more than a typical undergraduate adventure.[3]

More interesting than my comments, however, will be those of Dowson, himself. Symons wrote in the article: 'he is of a complete indifference to these things, as I shall assure myself over again before these lines are printed,' and he did so assure himself as the following letter from Dowson indicates:

le 5 Juliet [*sic*] 1896

Pont-Aven

My dear Symons,

My thanks for your charming letter & the article, à propos of myself & my work. You are right in assuming my complete indifference as to what things may be said of me over yonder, & I am content to be found of sufficient interest personally, to be the subject of your chronique. Would you, however, mind, toning down certain phrases on the *3rd* page of your proof which I return forthwith to you—sentences which would—if the veil of your article were penetrated—give an erroneous & too lurid account of me: for have I not been peacefully rusticating these five months en pleine campagne? The sentence 'Abroad in the *shadier* quarters of foreign cities etc down to "Gay" to him' is the one which I have in my mind & suggests the too hopelessly disreputable. *Could you, without spoiling your article,* change that sentence into an expression of the fact that my wanderings in foreign cities are a result of my chronic restlessness—for indeed I have long since outgrown mine old 'curious love of the sordid', & am grown the most pastoral of men? I should be grateful if you would do this, not so much for my own feelings, as for the benefit of sundry of my friends, who might otherwise be needlessly pained (as for instance Image, who heard exaggerated rumours of my life in Paris & was at the pains to write a most kind grieved and paternal letter).

If at the same time you would suppress a too alcoholic reference to the cabman's shelter—(for the 'refused admittance' was to outsiders generally & not personal) substitute 'readier means of oblivion' or some such phrase for 'oblivion of alcohols [*sic*]', & if you *could* possibly find a less ignoble word than 'very dilapidated', there is nothing in your article which I have any objection to your publishing.

It is always of curious interest to get any genuine idea of the manner in which others see you, & I am fortunate in my chronicler. I am especially charmed with the sympathy & tact with which you touch on what you rightly call my 'supreme sensation'. And for your conclusion I take off my hat to the compliment—the 'genius' is perhaps too partial & beaucoup trop flatteur, but, as no one is better aware than myself, I have always had, alas! too much of that 'swift, disastrous & suicidal energy' which destroyed our dear & incomparable Verlaine.

You will, probably, have seen some of my reviews. I foresee that I am to dispute the honour with you of being the most abused versifier in England, and I am flattered at the position. It is curious how uniformly the average reviewer will complain of your offering him violets because they are not cream-cheese, when doubtless if you bring him cream-cheese, he clamours for violets. And I hope you read the egregious remarks of the *Daily Courier*, who complained that I did not write patriotic platitudes which did not scan. Yet they have always their Austin, & his praise of *filibustiers*. But these reviews are really a joy to me.

I am daily expecting the announcement of Smithers' voyage here; perhaps, you will come with him. There have been charming people, & pretty & agreeable women here, but lately they have thinned out a little. It will be only too full, however, in a week or two. Have you seen the 'Centaure', a new French review which my friends Pierre Louys & Jean de Tinan have inaugurated with Henri de Regnier on the model of the 'Savoy'? Davray, as you doubtless know, is writing about ourselves, Yeats & Johnson in various places. The latest review *des jeunes* 'La Revue Sentimentale' is to publish a translation of one of my poems. I will send you the no. when it appears.

John Gray has sent me his new book 'Spiritual Poems'. I can not determine whether his mysticism is sincere or merely a pose—but I begin to think it is the former. I am glad you like my 'Donne' study.[4] I read & admired your 'Lucy Newcome' but, frankly, found it a little cold & impersonal. Your work which with your poems, fascinates me the most are those little studies & sketches, such as 'Dieppe' & 'Bertha' which are always exquisite & always personal, which in fact nobody but yourself can write. Let me hear from you when you have them.

Always Yours

ERNEST DOWSON[5]

Symons has not altogether played fair in his modification of 'very dilapidated' to 'somewhat dilapidated': it is quite obviously the word 'dilapidated' itself to which Dowson, understandably, objects.

Can one accept the truth of a portrait which its subject has accepted, bearing in mind the extent to which he desired alterations? Or would it be simple-minded to do so? Is it really the case that Dowson just does not care what is written about him? He evidently does care concerning what is said of his *work;* he also does not wish to appear 'too alcoholic' but does not object to 'readier means of oblivion' which is obvious in its implication; he does not like to be depicted as 'too hopelessly disreputable' and the phrase 'not so much for my own feeling' suggests that he does have some feeling. He is not really consistent for he begins by agreeing about his complete indifference to what is said. The sentence which, with all the politeness, really does convict Symons of distortion is: 'sentences which would . . . give an erroneous and too lurid account of me.' Nevertheless, though Symons' article must appear to the general reader to be tactless in the extreme, it is apparent that both Dowson and Symons do not place that value upon tact which the ordinary person tends to. The letter quoted is most probably, as Mr. Munro[6] notes, the one to which Longaker refers (p. 221):

> . . . Suffering, and detached as he was from his friends, Dowson was by no means indifferent to such cruel statements concerning his personal affairs and the oblivion which would soon overtake him. He was too ill and dispirited at the time to strike back, and furthermore there was little of the polemic in his nature when it came to such deeply affecting matters; but Yeats and others have reported that he wrote a letter of protest in which he stated that his life was not devoid of industry.

We have seen that it is not exactly a letter of protest and also that it was written in returning the proofs of the article, facts which remove an appreciable layer of discredit from the image of Symons. I find it impossible, however, to draw any fast conclusions, even from his letter, as to Dowson's true reaction. My own conclusion, which is tentative, is that Dowson himself does not really know what to feel about the matter and has, by the defence system which sometimes operates in those whom circumstances threaten to overtax, entered a phase of unco-ordinated thinking such as will prevent too vivid a picture of his real circumstances from confronting him. I think, too, that he is tremendously pleased to be classed with Verlaine, whose life was of course not impeccable, and that the immense flattery of this (to his mind) may well have overridden other objections which he might have felt. I believe that many well-intentioned supporters of Dowson *contra* Symons do not sufficiently realize that neither of these men was exactly eager to appear as a bourgeois model of virtue: they preferred to resemble their idols. In 1915, Symons wrote in the *North American Review:*

> Few of the idealists I have known have been virtuous—that is to say, they have chosen their virtues after a somewhat haphazard plan of their own; some of them have loved absinthe, others dirt, all idleness; but why expect everything at once? Have we, who lack ideas and ideals, enough of solid virtues to put into balance against these weighty abstractions?[7]

(And I think we may be sure that Symons does not really include himself in that 'we'.) In all of Symons' portraiture it is necessary to keep in mind the prevalence of this Bohemian *mystique* which never really lost its hold over him. This will be the more necessary when we turn now to the revised and lengthened version of the *Savoy* article which, after Dowson's death, Symons contributed to the *Fortnightly Review*. It was used again as the memoir in *The Poems of Ernest Dowson* in Symons' edition of 1905. To save space and time I shall reproduce only those parts of the Memoir which were not in the *Savoy* article, and only those relevant to this discussion[8]:

> I cannot remember my first meeting with Ernest Dowson. It may have been in 1891, at one of the meetings of the Rhymers' Club, in an upper room of the 'Cheshire Cheese' . . . [p. viii].
>
> [Symons obviously could not mention the Rhymers in the *Savoy* article without prejudicing the anonymity—however factitious that anonymity may have been.]
>
> . . . The daughter of a refugee, I believe of good family, reduced to keeping a humble restaurant in a foreign quarter of London, she listened to his verses, smiled charmingly, under her mother's eyes, on his two years' courtship, and at the end of two years

> married the waiter instead. Did she ever realize more than the obvious part of what was being offered to her, in this shy and eager devotion? Did it ever mean very much to her to have made and to have killed a poet? [p. xiii].
>
> . . . Meanwhile she and the mother knew that the fragile young man who dined there so quietly every day was apt to be quite another sort of person after he had been three hours outside. It was only when his life seemed to have been irretrievably ruined that Dowson quite deliberately abandoned himself to that craving for drink, which was doubtless lying in wait for him in his blood, as consumption was also; it was only latterly, when he had no longer any interest in life, that he really wished to die. But I have never known him when he could resist either the desire or the consequences of drink. Sober he was the most gentle, in manner the most gentlemanly of men; unselfish to a fault, to the extent of weakness; a delightful companion, charm itself. Under the influence of drink, he became almost literally insane, certainly quite irresponsible. He fell into furious and unreasoning passions; a vocabulary unknown to him at other times sprang up like a whirlwind; he seemed always about to commit some act of absurd violence. Along with that forgetfulness came other memories. As long as he was conscious of himself, there was but one woman for him in the world, and for her he had an infinite tenderness and an infinite respect. When that face faded from him, he saw all the other faces, and he saw no more difference than between sheep and sheep. [p. xv].
>
> . . . His father, when he died, left him in possession of an old dock, where for a time he lived in a mouldering house, in that squalid part of the East End which he came to know so well, and to feel so strangely at home in. He drank the poisonous liquors of those pot-houses which swarm about the docks; he drifted about in whatever company came in his way; he let heedlessness develop into a curious disregard of personal tidiness. In Paris, Les Halles took the place of the docks. At Dieppe, where I saw so much of him one summer, he discovered strange, squalid haunts about the harbour, where he made friends with amazing inn-keepers, and got into rows with the fishermen who came in to drink after midnight. At Brussels, where I was with him at the time of the Kermesse, he flung himself into all that riotous Flemish life, with a zest for what was most sordidly riotous in it. It was his own way of escape from life. [p. xvi].

There follows a sympathetic consideration of Dowson's tragedy and a just and discerning critique of his verse, recognizing its high merit. The assertion that Dowson could not have developed further in his poetry is perhaps unwarrantable, however.

It would, of course, be absurd to accuse the girl of killing the poet. But Symons does not accuse her; he merely speculates wonderingly upon what has, without her understanding, come about. It is *not* strange that Dowson should feel 'at home' in his home, even if it is in the East End: the Dock had been a solid family business; it was not 'mouldering' except in so far as custom was falling off, and one of Dowson's occupations had been to keep the accounts there. Plarr described the Dock-house as 'delightful'.[9]

That Symons believed in what he wrote, and I am thinking particularly of the references to drink and drabs, seems evident from a letter to his bride-to-be, Rhoda Bowser, written in February 1900 concerning the *Fortnightly* article:

> It is so difficult to know what one may and what one may not say, isn't it. I want to be quite frank and yet I don't want to say too much. *Isn't* it difficult? But I know one thing: I shall write something which would please him, if he could read it now. He had almost a pathetic admiration for me and for everything I did: I always looked upon it as one of the things that most really honoured me. And it happened that I was the only one among the younger men whose work he cared for.[10]

The last statement is not supported by some of the letters to Plarr which I have quoted in preceding chapters, where Dowson has praised poems of Johnson and Plarr but not mentioned Symons. As to the statement that he will 'write something which would please him,' it seems impossible to conclude in the light of Dowson's letter which we have read, whether Symons is genuinely insensitive to the implications of Dowson's remarks or anxious to deceive himself as much as Rhoda. The antithesis between being 'quite frank' and 'I shall write something which would please him', suggests to me that he intends to salve his conscience for being 'franker' than he knows Dowson would like by 'writing something which would please': that is, about his verse. He apparently, then, does not believe that his earlier remarks about Dowson put things in an 'erroneous and lurid' light. But he knows that Dowson thought this to be so and therefore, however highly he may appraise the verse, he intends doing the dead man a disservice. Why? I suggest, again tentatively, that the answer lies in that slight inhumanity which the doctrines of the aesthetic school tend, by their exaltation of art above common humanity, to beget. Symons can only see one objective, the impressionistic rendering into careful prose of those features of Dowson's life which will serve to build the picture which he desires of an English Decadent; his fault is one that is central to the Decadent Movement—it does not distinguish art from life. But there is no *evidence* that the gist of Symons' remarks about drink and women is untrue, I hasten to add.

In a paper read to the Royal Society of Literature in London on 9 March, 1938, Mr. John Gawsworth examined 'The Dowson Legend' and demonstrated convincingly how the Symons article of 1900, and the same account as preface in 1906, was consciously or unconsciously absorbed by many writers of all degrees and reproduced, often with even more lurid highlights, by them in their writings about the poet, the borrowing often being evidenced by the exact repetition of Symons' words and phrases.[10] Among the extenders of the 'legend' in this way are included: Mr. Talcott Williams, Frank Harris, Mr. Louis Untermeyer, Bernard Muddiman, W. B. Yeats, Mrs. Gertrude Atherton, Osbert Burdett, Le Gallienne, Grant Richards, J. Lewis May and Vincent O'Sullivan. The other aspect of the 'legend' which Mr. Gawsworth treated, was the belief, started apparently by Mr. Mosher, that the girl Adelaide was 'Cynara', but I am not concerned with that here. The extraordinary weakness of Mr. Gawsworth's defence does not seem to have been noted in the excitement of vindicating one reputation at the expense of a not undistinguished dozen or so. The mere fact that a writer on Dowson uses a phrase from Symons is taken as dismissing that writer's claim to any original veracity forthwith. Indeed, poor Mr. Guy Thorne who, in *T.P.'s Weekly* of 11 July, 1913, recalled seeing the poet 'towards the end of his short and tragic life . . . pale, emaciated, in clothes that were almost ragged,' is dismissed out of hand, presumably as a liar, even though he has not used here a phrase from Symons. We may read that Dowson in his last days was 'pale' and 'emaciated' and 'almost ragged' in the account of one of Mr. Gawsworth's defence witnesses, Ernest Rhys (see below, p. 132). Then again, the only witnesses for the opposite point of view of Dowson's life are Edgar Jepson, Victor Plarr and —through not saying anything about the disreputable—Ernest Rhys. Jepson, in fact—as Gawsworth points out—came early to the defence of Dowson's respectability. The reader of this study has had a fair sample of Jepson's thinking in his later years from the excerpt concerning Decadence. Gawsworth does not quote fully from his 'defendants' and I give all that he has stated for Jepson:

> Mr. Edgar Jepson, properly taking exception to this [an article by the American critic, Talcott Williams, using Symons], protested against it, and its source, in *The Academy* of 2 November, 1907, in an article, 'The Real Ernest Dowson', declaring that his friend had not, in fact, been 'a rather disagreeable wastrel'. [Symons wrote no such phrase, of course.] This refutation he accompanied with corrections of not a few of Mr. Symons' statements, and an additional page of first-hand reminiscence, for he could claim that during two years Dowson and he had

spent 'on the average four evenings a week together'. In 1933, after much injurious matter in literary and journalistic memoirs had appeared, Mr. Jepson, in his 'Memories of a Victorian', returned once more to his criticism of Mr. Symons' phrases, and this time dealt with them more fully: 'When', he writes in this volume, 'Mr. Symons states that Dowson felt strangely at home in that squalid part of the East End, Stepney, drinking "the poisonous liquors of those pot-houses which swarm about the docks", he is writing nonsense. Dowson always made the greatest possible haste, a daily haste, to get out of the East End to the society of his kind. . . . No less nonsensical is Mr. Symons' statement that Dowson loves the sordid . . . In his hour of prosperity . . . Dowson wore a frock-coat from Saville Row and a masterpiece of Mr. Henry Heath [i.e. a top hat], and more beautifully dressed than any other poet I have known, was fit to walk Bond Street. . . . With regard to his drinking, on which Mr. Symons lays such stress, during the years we perused London together Dowson would get drunk now and then. But who did not? Nevertheless for weeks together he would be sober enough.' [pp. 96–97].

Concerning this it is possible to ask: how does Jepson know that Dowson *always* 'made the greatest possible haste to get out of the East End'? It is clear from other matter in my study that Dowson generally did, but there may have been occasions of which Jepson knew nothing. As to Dowson's loving the sordid, the letter of Dowson's from France, which I quoted, contains the sentence: 'I have long since outgrown mine old "curious love of the sordid".' Clearly, Jepson knew nothing of that phase. Jepson's faith in top-hats is extraordinary. Did he never read *The Picture of Dorian Gray*, or, to put it less dramatically, does he imagine that such garments confer an indisputable seal of rectitude? And, as a defence of Dowson's drinking habits, the evidence of Jepson is by no means very persuasive: how should we think of a stranger, for example, of whom it was said 'for weeks together he would be sober enough' (not sober, mind, but '*sober enough*')?

Gawsworth relates how Victor Plarr published his *Reminiscences etc.* of Dowson in 1914 as another attempt to defend him from the ever-growing 'legend'. He admits that the drawback to this venture was the expurgation to which Plarr subjected the quoted letters. All that Gawsworth finds to say about Plarr's book is:

> And though Plarr stated as emphatically as Mr. Jepson that Dowson was no foul-mouthed inebriate (that misconstruction of his character being 'generated chiefly in the closely allied consciences of America and of British Nonconformity'), and

> emphasized, to the point of redundancy, that the poet's acts were 'far, very far, from the depths of lurid dissipation that is being allowed to cover his good fame, unless it be rescued betimes', his assertions alone were hardly sufficient to turn the balance of opinion. [pp. 99–100.]

Now, to begin with, I have always believed it to be an unfair practice to make the kind of violent paraphrase which has here the effect of crediting Symons with having called Dowson a 'foul-mouthed inebriate'. Then, what is the point of the parenthesis about Nonconformity, quoted from Plarr? The implication is obviously that only a puritanical mind would have found Dowson's language foul and his sobriety impaired. The further implication is that such a one was Symons. He had, you will recall from the preceding chapter, strict Methodist parents. How anyone who knew as much of Symons as Plarr, a Rhymer, must have known, could even think of regarding him as puritanical I leave the reader to judge from my account of that poet-critic. Nevertheless, Plarr's point may be taken: he believes that Dowson was not luridly dissipated (how dissipated is that?) and not at all as Symons describes him. Even if Plarr had made his case efficiently, as one may see that he has not, we have, as Gawsworth laments, simply this view as compared with Symons'. Who is to say which of these knew the whole picture of Dowson's life? Probably neither did. All that remains of Gawsworth's defence is a reference to Rhys, who:

> ... in his entertaining 'Everyman Remembers', 1931, uninfluenced by his reading, adds nothing to the myth, but writes of Dowson scrupulously and with respect and regard. [p. 104.]

One may also comment that he is 'uninfluenced' as much by Plarr and Jepson, then, as by Symons, and that he *subtracts* nothing *from* the myth.

Longaker, in his biography (p. 56), wrote:

> ... Plarr's own kindly nature helped him to recall the early years of his friendship with Dowson in a manner perhaps more penetrating than that of those whose recollections of Dowson's young manhood are tinged with the shadows of his later years.

I must admit that Longaker is not referring here to dissipation and so forth, but to the strains and stresses which marked Dowson's later years. Nevertheless, I think this comment would account for many of the differences which comprise the problem of the 'two Dowsons'.

Gawsworth did not complete the quotation from Jepson. Jepson continued:

> The craving for liquor which at times came upon him was a malady natural to a man with the nerves of a consumptive. Neither he nor Lionel Johnson could stand the strain of life, and at times liquor alone could give them relief. Naturally a couple of whiskies and sodas came to have as intoxicating effect on them as half a dozen on the average man.[12]

Finally, with regard to women, Longaker—who has sifted most of the available evidence in compiling his biography—wrote:

> . . . That he recognized the uses of sexual love can be proved more adequately than in most cases. In fact, this phase of Dowson's life is far plainer than many which propriety need not slight. . . . Sherard recalls that Dowson, in his last years while sharing his rooms in Paris, could not deny his urge for female companionship of the looser sort, and would bring ladies of the night into his quarters without showing the slightest embarrassment.[13]

Although Gawsworth mentions Sherard's *Twenty Years in Paris* (London, 1905), and brackets it, as it were, with the list of those who every year 'employed themselves in the service of the "romantic legend"', he has not a word of refutation about it.

To conclude: Gawsworth has not succeeded in showing that the disreputable facts which have been presented by Symons and others concerning Dowson's life are false. What has emerged from the sequence of contradictory material which I have presented is that there were many, of whom Jepson, Plarr and, later, Gawsworth were some, who felt that Symons, in spite of the pleasant character which he ascribed to the sober Dowson, had excessively highlighted what might be called the vicious Dowson. One of the basic conflicts here, bedevilling the issue, is between 'Victorian morality', with its polite disregard of 'what the eye doesn't see', and the Decadent—one may say 'modern', I think—attitude, which values a somewhat brutal but honest exposure of man's appetites more highly than a surface respectability. The defenders of Dowson could not, and still cannot, see that Symons and Dowson—as disciples of Verlaine and sharers in the Decadent Movement—did not share the conventional moral standards of the day: they had passed beyond Ruskin's insistence on a *moral* aesthetic and did not subscribe to the whole tenor of the writings of Pater which also insist upon a moral code in aestheticism as I shall later indicate.

Plarr's 'Nonconformist' critic, Arthur Symons, wrote the following in an unpublished paper, 'Sex and Aversion':

> In certain night vigils, or in waking dreams, I remember not without some of Baudelaire's cynical amusement and sardonic

irony, the various well-known men who—being aware not only of my verses, but of the fact of the immoral life I was certainly then leading, that I was a danger to Society—deliberately snubbed me in the street. . . .[14]

Dr. Russell M. Goldfarb has illustrated the extent to which the original account of Dowson by Symons has continued to be the main source, to the present day, for most critics' accounts of Dowson's life, despite the effects of Gawsworth.[15] He does not, however, produce any new evidence for the 'defence' of Dowson, and he draws upon Longaker's biography only for what would seem to support his argument; for instance: 'To name him decadent tells only a part of the story, a part which has been sufficiently emphasized' (Longaker, p. vii). I would agree with Dr. Longaker and Dr. Goldfarb in this remark but it is still not usable as a defence of Dowson, and Dr. Goldfarb does not refer to those parts of Longaker which I have already quoted. Again, Dr. Goldfarb's understanding of the term *decadence* seems to me too limited. His general conclusion that it is the work and not the man which should receive our attention is such as one can hardly disagree with (why then does Dr. Goldfarb write on the man?), but 'the common reader' *will* ask about the man, and it is someone's, the biographer's, task to strive for an accurate portrait.

The amount of space which I have devoted to 'the Dowson Legend' may seem disproportionate to the reader unaware of the amount of effort already expended by others in trying to do an impossible service to Dowson's private name which would have caused him at most a shy grin of wry amusement. In the chapter which follows it will be with the work and sober and delightful converse of Dowson that I shall be principally concerned and not with his unguarded hours.

REFERENCES

1 'A Study of John Addington Symonds', *Fortnightly Review*, February 1924, pp. 228–239.

2 Arthur Symons, *The Café Royal and Other Essays* (London, 1923), p. 8.

3 See Longaker, pp. 42–43.

4 The short story, 'The Dying of Francis Donne.'

5 *The Letters of Ernest Dowson*, ed. Desmond Flower and Henry Maas (London, 1967), pp. 371–372.

6 A copy of this letter was first published by Professor John H. Munro: 'A Previously Unpublished Letter from Ernest Dowson to Arthur Symons,' *Études Anglaisis* XVII (1964), 3, pp. 285–287.

7 May 1915, pp. 745–746.

8 I quote from the 7th Edition (London, 1917).

9 Plarr, p. 32.

[10] Lhombreaud, p. 174.

[11] *Essays by Divers Hands*, XVII (Royal Society of Literature, London, 1938): John Gawsworth, 'The Dowson Legend', pp. 93–123.

[12] See Longaker, p. 221.

[13] Longaker, p. 154.

[14] Lhombreaud, p. 257.

[15] Russell M. Goldfarb, 'The Dowson Legend Today,' SEL IV, (Autumn 1964), p. 653–662.

CHAPTER VII

Ernest Dowson

IN March, 1888, Ernest Dowson left Queen's College, Oxford, having decided that he did not wish to stay the three-year course for a degree. He had been an undergraduate for five terms, having matriculated at the age of nineteen. He appears to have been admitted to Queen's on the strength of an unusually broad knowledge of French and Latin, being somewhat defective in the other general subjects of an English schoolboy's curriculum.[1] The principal reason for his rather unusual educational background was the frequent travelling to the South of France, and sojourning there, which was necessary for his father's weak health. Ernest had been unable to obtain regular schooling but instead had had its place supplied by a variety of tutors, one of whom had encouraged an interest in the substance of the classics.[1]

The photograph of Ernest Dowson at Oxford (Longaker, facing p. 32) shows us an unremarkable figure in a Queen's blazer and striped flannels. His adoption of this attire shows that he was not impervious to the collegiate atmosphere nor hostile to it. It seems that he had lacked an ordinary boy's friendships, owing to his unsettled domicilage, and that after an initial period of shyness and adjustment, he became happy in the company of W. R. Thomas (to whom we owe the account of his Oxford years),[2] Arthur Moore and Sam Smith. The four students formed a luncheon club at which they took turns to speak on a chosen topic. After leaving Oxford, Dowson was to collaborate with Arthur Moore in the writing of two novels: *A Comedy of Masks* (London, 1893) and *Adrian Rome* (London, 1899). Sam Smith has been mentioned earlier in this study as a correspondent of Dowson's. He translated, at a later date, the *Lysistrata*.

Dowson's interest in Latin literature was not that of a scholar, as Lionel Johnson's was for instance, and it would appear to have drawn attention more for the curious phenomenon of its unschooled and voluntary delight, rather than for the more usual skill and discipline in pursuing the well-worn track to the examination hall. His favourite Latin writers, while he was at Oxford, were Horace, Catullus and Propertius, and his letters reveal a slightly later acknowledgement of the greatness of Virgil. Longaker writes:

> The truth of the matter was that his Latin was by no means exact. His prose compositions, Thomas recalled, were done *currente calamo*, and rarely found favour among those who supervised his study. [p. 34.]

His approach to this literature was to extract whatever he found stimulating to the imagination, an approach to some extent comparable to that of Ezra Pound in the succeeding generation.

In French literature his favourite poet was Baudelaire, his favourite novelist Zola, while the other writers whom he admired were Gautier, Musset and Maupassant.[3] He had none of that reading in English literature (Dickens, Scott, Thackeray etc.) which was part of the general legacy of an English education, but chose instead the then not widely read Jacobean dramatists and the more widely read Jacobean poets. Of Americans he admired Henry James and Edgar Allan Poe.

He is reported as having returned for his second Oxford year with a noticeably diminished gaiety[4] but no reasons for this have been positively advanced. We know that his father was in the grip of a business failure at the Dock and of ever-declining health. The outlook of many of the young men at Oxford was pessimistic,[5] partaking of the belief in the heedless Immanent Will which we find expressed in Hardy's novels. Nature was seen as unsympathetic, as 'red in tooth and claw', while humanity was viewed with some distrust and aversion. The pessimism of undergraduates does not often interfere with their pleasures or gaiety, and their later involvement in the world's activity generally displaces most of their *weltschmertz*. The man who makes thought and feeling his life's study, however, as a poet presumably does, is often not relieved of this burden of his youthful conscience—he must see through what others have been content to shrug off as a philosophy incompatible with a successful material existence. As to gaiety, indeed, there are two gaieties: the one is that of Wordsworth contemplating the daffodils; the other is that suggested by the name of the Gaiety Theatre. Of the gaiety which springs from pessimism Dowson had his full share.

Returning to London from Oxford, while Lionel Johnson (whom he had met there occasionally) went on to win honours,

Dowson occupied himself by day with the account-books of Bridge Dock and hastened early each evening to the social delights of Henekey's Tavern, The Cock and other resorts, near Fleet Street, of young men about town.[6] In such ramblings he met Charles Sayle ('C' of Johnson's *Winchester Letters*) who in turn introduced him to the man who was to be his best and steadiest friend—Victor Plarr. Plarr spent most of his life as librarian to The Royal College of Surgeons but was also, as has appeared, a poet. He had rooms in Great Russell Street,[7] a conveniently central location of which Dowson made use on those nights when Limehouse seemed too distant and the hour too late. Plarr has described the young Dowson as '. . . singularly fresh, young, eager, sympathetic, his charming face unscathed by any serious sorrows or dissipations . . .'[8] and as '. . . the pleasant youth, who played billiards punctually at six o'clock every evening and smoked rather vile Vevey cigars. . . .'[9] By 1890 Dowson had obtained a part-time post as assistant editor of *The Critic*, work which he appears to have enjoyed but which was short-lived since this periodical only survived, through five numbers, until March.

Dowson's friendship with Johnson was renewed and strengthened when Johnson, as has been related, came to live in 'Fitzroy' in 1890. Johnson's admission to the Roman Catholic Church in June, 1891, was followed by Dowson's later that year. It is not clear, however, who influenced Dowson's decision. Plarr was not pleased with what he considered a purely emotional gesture:

> He came to me rather excitedly, and yet shook hands with weak indecision. His hesitating hand-shake, alas! always betrayed a sorrowful fatigue. 'I have been admitted,' he said, but he seemed disappointed, for the heavens had not fallen, nor had a sign been vouchsafed. The priest who had admitted him had done so quite casually and had seemed bored. Afterwards, it seemed to me, he forgot about his religion with surprising alacrity. Only his poetry bears witness to his romantic admiration of a creed, which, after all, he shares with many Protestants and Agnostics.
>
> Respecting sincere Catholics as I do, I was keenly annoyed with his conversion—with this kind of conversion. It was comparable to the way in which our clever young men of today, with no knowledge of biology, folk-lore, or the rationale of English constitutional history, become Socialists. But I held my tongue. Our literary life is a long reticence at best.[10]

(It is difficult, in face of the spate of memoirs of the 'nineties, to suppress a wry smile at Plarr's last sentence here.) Plarr may be right by his own lights; but in God's house (however we envisage

God) there are 'many mansions'. Catholicism provided for Dowson a receptacle for his mystical sense, as Magic did for Yeats. Both were opposed at this time to the 'science' Plarr enjoins, which however necessary to Socialism is not necessarily an indispensable credential for a Christian conversion. That neither Johnson nor Dowson was a Christian in the true theological sense is indisputable: neither submitted his will.

In 1891, Lionel Johnson wrote a definition of Decadence:

> In English, *décadence* and the literature thereof, means this: the period, at which passion, or romance, or tragedy, or sorrow, or any other form of activity or of emotion, must be refined upon, and curiously considered, for literary treatment: an age of afterthought, of reflection. Hence come one great virtue, and one great vice: the virtue of much and careful meditation upon life. its emotions and its incidents: the vice of over subtility and of affectation, when thought thinks upon itself, and when emotions become entangled with the consciousness of them.[11]

The poetry and prose of Ernest Dowson may, by this and by my earlier tentative definition, be seen as Decadent. Most of Dowson's stories (for example 'A Case of Conscience', 'Apple Blossom in Brittany', 'The Statute of Limitations') concern men whose lives become tragical through impossible love for

> . . . the dainty figure of a little girl, a child of fifteen but seeming younger . . .
> . . . This child with her fragility, her face of a youthful Madonna . . .

such as 'Countess Marie of the Angels' was.[12]

One, perhaps the best—certainly the most moving—of Dowson's prose-pieces (they are often more sketches than 'stories') treats of a different subject: what it is like to be aware of approaching death. This, 'The Dying of Francis Donne', was written when the by then consumptive poet's own memories of love, which had been 'refined upon and curiously considered, for literary treatment,' were being overlaid by his awareness of his own imminent disintegration.

In Dowson's poetry, love—nearly always for an idealized woman—is really the one theme. There is then what one may call the 'counter-theme' of withdrawal, of rejection of the world in which such ideal love can never be realized. Katherine Brégy wrote:

> We have spoken of him as the poet of a single passion—the passion of his hopeless love. But having the grace to be a poet, he transmuted this love into a symbol of all remote and inaccessible loveliness: of the Ideal which changes not. . . .[13]

By 'his hopeless love', however, I fear that Miss Brégy was referring to his love for the small girl, Adelaide. This conception is too limited; the ideal love existed in Dowson's verse and prose before he came to know the London café-owner's daughter. It is much more probable that his love for the girl was an offshoot of his poetical imaginings than *vice versa*.

Dowson's most celebrated poem, 'Non sum qualis eram bonae sub regno Cynarae', makes use of the situation presented by a Horatian Ode based upon the 'Cynthia' of Propertius—a situation which Symons also treated in 'To One in Alienation', and which inspired several of the poets of the 'nineties in England and France. The reason for the popularity of this theme is evident when it is considered as a metaphorical statement of the Decadent attitude. The situation is that of one in the arms of a 'bought' lover being stricken with sadness at the remembrance of a lost innocent love. I use the word 'sadness' advisedly, for it is not remorse that is felt. I need perhaps hardly elaborate the metaphor as one of ideality *versus* reality. Dowson's poem is rightly seen as one of the finest expressions of the Decadent spirit in England. Victor Plarr wrote:

> There is a singular, a poignant parallelism between the great and prolonged *cri de coeur* of the old Roman [Propertius], and the modern's sorrowful lament, as expressed, for instance, in his Cynara poem, the boldness of which is august with the spirit of antiquity, as though the pagan had passed into and inspired the unhappy lad of the day before yesterday.[14]

The Parnassian restraint which more often characterizes Dowson's verse is banished in this poem. What is remarkable in all of his verse is the ability to use age-old symbols—roses, wine, violets, vine-leaves, red fruit—while seldom becoming trite or stale. He is successful, as Professor Tillotson has pointed out, because of his exactitude in their use:

> . . . in such a line as
>
> *Vine leaves, kisses and bay*
>
> he is not only trying to assemble beautiful words but is saying something exact. The line contains a symbol each for wine, women and song. Dowson derives from Swinburne, but he does not snatch at the first things that come to a poet's eyes for the sake of saying them divinely, does not transform a modicum of complex but limited impressions into a thousand lines of lyric. He may be dreadfully intent on writing poetry that shall be flawless as verbal music, and that music may be of an exacting and subtle kind, but all this is only half his activity. Dowson does give minute attention to working over and over his lines, to

punctuation, to placing capital letters as a refinement for indicating accent; and yet, beside all this, he is putting in an equal amount of work on improving his meaning. He succeeds in the use of forms like the villanelle because he can write lines which are substantial enough to bear repetition, or to make minute variation worth while.

Tillotson also writes:

> More important for the way poetry has developed since, are Dowson's experiments and achievements in rhythm. In this he stands beside Mr. Yeats. In the 'Trembling of the Veil' Mr. Yeats calls 'Innisfree' the first poem he had written 'with anything in its rhythm of my own music. . . . I had begun to loosen rhythm as an escape from rhetoric'. This loosening of the rhythm has been found important by later poets, Mr. Eliot using late Elizabethan blank verse as a further solvent. Dowson's loosening was mainly carried out in the alexandrine, which in previous English verse had been either the hexameter or the six-iambic-footed line, the alexandrine, which Pope compared to a wounded snake. Dowson gave the English alexandrine the flexibility of the French alexandrine: e.g.
>
> And I was desolate and sick of an old passion. . . .
>
> The loosening of rhythm connected Dowson with Mr. Eliot, some of whose many roots may be found gripping Dowson's best poem, 'Non sum qualis eram bonae sub regno Cynarae'.[15]

I wrote earlier of Dowson's 'counter-theme' of withdrawal. This appears in poems such as 'To One in Bedlam':

> *. . . Better than mortal flowers,*
> *Thy moon-kissed roses seem: better than love or sleep,*
> *The star-crowned solitude of thine oblivious hours!*[16] [p. 46]

and in 'Nuns of the Perpetual Adoration', where the sentiments imputed to the nuns are hardly Christian, the convent being seen as a refuge from a sick world:

> *Outside, the world is wild and passionate;*
> *Man's weary laughter and his sick despair*
> *Entreat at their impenetrable gate:*
> *They heed no voices in their dream of prayer.* [p. 42]

The nuns' mood is that of Ecclesiastes—not of the gospels. But these two poems form part of what I consider to be Dowson's best work, where the sentiment is unforced, the style limpid and of a delicate grace. To a very large extent Dowson's style images what he venerates—a fragile, sensitive, reposeful beauty.

Dowson's poetry could be at times, if not exactly gay, at least as debonnaire as the beauty of Manon whom he addresses in 'Rondeau'. This poem is exactly opposite in sentiment to 'Cynara':

RONDEAU

Ah, Manon, say, why is it we
Are one and all so fain of thee?
Thy rich red beauty debonnaire
In very truth is not more fair,
Than the shy grace and purity
That clothe the maiden maidenly;
Her gray eyes shine more tenderly
And not less bright than thine her hair,
Ah, Manon, say!
Expound, I pray, the mystery
Why wine-stained lip and languid eye,
And most unsaintly Maenad air,
Should move us more than all the rare
White roses of virginity?
Ah, Manon, say! [p. 131]

Dowson tried his hand at a great variety of metrical forms, being in this a disciple of Banville, who sought to free French verse from the *rigor mortis* of defunct classicism. Experiment is an essential part of a poet's apprenticeship, of course, and this experiment will extend to more than prosody—will be also with moods and subjects. The more impressionable, literary and lacking in individuality a poet is, the more derivative his forms and subjects will be. Individuality may appear with maturity and the 'personal note' which I have referred to in Dowson's best verse was, I feel, the result of such a maturing. It is Dowson's tragedy, as a poet, that maturity and death appeared upon the scene together—his muse dying some months before his body. It is not simply that death cut off his poetic destiny: the sickness which led to it affected his spirit during his closing years, preventing his full flowering. His second slim book of verse, *Decorations: In Verse and Prose*, which appeared in 1899, about six months before the poet's death on 23 February, 1900, revealed little development and some of its finest things, 'A Last Word', for example, had been written long before even the first volume (*Verses*, 1896).

Victor Plarr wrote of *Decorations:*

> . . . to me, it marks an extreme falling-away of the poet's powers. It is full of lassitude and sorrowfulness, as of a man who has done with the world and is dying disillusioned.[17]

One very curious aspect of Dowson's work is the way in which so often his poetry seems to have anticipated his future experience. Thus while still at Oxford he composed *Sonnets, Of A Little Girl* (number IV), which was published in *London Society*, Vol. 50, in November 1886. It was not until several years later that Dowson met Adelaide Foltinowicz, the little daughter of the Polish café proprietor in Soho. It is answerable that the poet's early fantasies and imaginings shaped his destiny. Jepson remarked that there was a cult of little girls at Oxford during the 'eighties. Undergraduate parties would take them out to tea. The daughter of the Dean of Christ Church comes immediately to mind. In Guy Harrison's list of Dowson's works appears an article, 'The Cult of the Child', which appeared anonymously in the short-lived periodical *The Critic*. Imagination and self-deception must play a part in every relationship of lovers; in the case of a poet such as Dowson it is probable that imagination played the largest part of all, the restaurant-keeper's daughter appearing as an incarnation of the notion of girlish innocence. It is an innocence, moreover, which the poet desires for himself, as much as in the beloved. He wishes to preserve a, as it were, virginal state of mind, to share in the refusal of Pater's 'Sebastian Van Storck' to become any one limited thing. Such an attitude led some young Oxford men of that time, and to some extent again in the 'twenties, when there was a brief resurgence of 'aestheticism', to say that a man was 'finished' at twenty-six. Certainly, Rhymers such as Johnson and Dowson seem to have lived most intensely before that age and to have been unable or unwilling to attempt that compromise with the grosser realities of existence which is perhaps an element in what we call maturity. Dowson wrote in Jepson's birthday book:

> The small things of life are odious to me, and the habit of them enslaves me; the great things of life are eternally attractive to me, but indolence and fear put them by.[18]

Verlaine's influence upon Dowson's work was not always beneficial, as he himself realized at times. He wrote to Victor Plarr:

> . . . I send you in return, my latest Versicles: the merest 'symbolism'; almost too slight for criticism! It's an attempt at mere sound verse, with scarcely the shadow of a scuse in it: or hardly that so much as a vague Verlainesque motion. It's an inferior production. . . .[19]

Villiers de L'Isle-Adam, Verlaine, and other French poets had decided that it was futile to write poetry addressed to a wide general public. In his preface to 'Dédicaces' (Paris, 1890) Verlaine wrote:

Ces quelques ballades et sonnets sont tout intimes et ne visent que quelques amis et bons camarades de l'auteur qui les leur *dédie* exclusivement, sans autre intention que de leur plaire.

In his collection of poems 'Silverpoints' (1893), John Gray followed Verlaine's practice of actually placing a personal dedication at the head of each poem. Dowson's *Verses* are similarly dedicated and the *Times* reviewer was moved to comment:

Mr Ernest Dowson labels each of the short pieces which make up his *Verses* as having been written specially for a particular person. Of this curious practice *Beata Solitudo, For Sam Smith* may be cited as a pleasing example. It must be rather alarming, however, for the friends of those mentioned to come across such a heading to a page as *Extreme Unction, For Lionel Johnson* or *A Requiem, For John Gray* when there is no reason to believe that the gentlemen in question are anything but alive and well.[20]

I would say that Dowson's adaptations of Verlaine and his Verlainesque poems are not his best work but are nevertheless skilful and effective; for a time Dowson found what seemed a mood and approach in sympathy with his own, and the influence of Verlaine remained with him. In his best work, however, Dowson attains a rhythm and a lyrical grace entirely his own. It may be, indeed, that to speak of Dowson's 'Verlainesque' poems is misleading, for it is not so much that Dowson owes to him any stylistic debt but simply that he was able to find an echo of his own mood of wistful apprehension of 'the bitter and the gay' in the French poet's verses. A comparison of Dowson's 'Autumnal' with Verlaine's celebrated 'Chanson d'Automne' may illustrate this affinity of mood rather than style:

AUTUMNAL

Pale amber sunlight falls across
The reddening October trees,
That hardly sway before a breeze
As soft as summer: summer's loss
Seems little, dear! on days like these!

Let misty autumn be our part!
The twilight of the year is sweet:
Where shadow and the darkness meet
Our love, a twilight of the heart
Eludes a little time's deceit.

Are we not better and at home
In dreamful Autumn, we who deem
No harvest joy is worth a dream?
A little while and night shall come,
A little while, then, let us dream.

Beyond the pearled horizons lie
Winter and night: awaiting these
We garner this poor hour of ease,
Until love turn from us and die
Beneath the drear November trees. [p. 74]

CHANSON D'AUTOMNE

Les sanglots longs
Des violons
De l'automne
Blessent mon coeur
D'une langeur
Monotone.

Tout suffocant
Et blême, quand
Sonne, l'heure,
Je me souviens
Des jours anciens
Et je pleure;

Et je m'en vais
Au vent mauvais
Qui m'emporte
Decà, delà,
Pareil à la
Feuille morte.

[Paul Verlaine, *Oeuvres Poétiques Complètes*, Librairie Gallimard, 1957, p. 56]

One poem which owes as much, perhaps, to Poe as to Verlaine, is 'Coronal', from which I shall quote the first verse:

Violets and leaves of vine,
Into a frail, fair wreath
We gather and entwine:
A wreath for Love to wear,
Fragrant as his own breath,
To crown his brow divine,
All day till night is near.
Violets and leaves of vine
We gather and entwine [p. 40]

We may infer that Dowson did not really think so harshly of this poem, for he placed it first in *Verses*. Arthur Symons recalled Dowson's saying that he considered the line 'The viol, the violet, and the vine' from Poe's poem 'The City in the Sea' one of the most beautiful in the English language. While an indebtedness to Poe is apparent in some of Dowson's technical devices, as in his poetry of almost pure incantation, Dowson has no share in the substitution of verbal excitement for rational content.

Dowson's dramatic fantasy *The Pierrot of the Minute* is a delightful trifle which William Theodore Peters encouraged him to write. Peters produced the one-act play at the Albert Hall Theatre, himself acting the Pierrot, early in 1893. In yet another form, Dowson dramatizes his 'single passion':

[THE LADY] ... *Remember me, who was compassionate,*
And opened for thee once, the ivory gate.
I come no more, thou shalt not see my face
When I am gone to mine exalted place:
Yet all thy days are mine, dreamer of dreams,
All silvered over with the moon's pale beams:
Go forth and seek in each fair face in vain,
To find the image of thy love again. [p. 179]

Although Dowson, like most poets, uses alliteration, he does not rely heavily upon it; it does not 'carry' the line to such an extent as to dominate it. This distinguishes him from Swinburne, to whom his debt, as has been noted, is obviously considerable but with whom he was often bracketed as a mere imitator. His use of Swinburnian metre makes him no more an imitator than was Whitman or Kipling. The absence of alliteration makes for a softness of tone and prevents the lines from galloping off ahead of the meaning or even abandoning meaning altogether—as often happens with Swinburne. Dowson appears, in his best poetry, always to achieve an exact fit of form and meaning or feeling. A good example of this is his use of the villanelle—an intricate form, of which Ezra Pound wrote:

> The villanelle even can, at its best, achieve the closest intensity, I mean when, as with Dowson, the refrains are an emotional fact, which the intellect, in the various gyrations of the poems, tries in vain and in vain to escape.[21]

This is true of the following:

VILLANELLE OF THE POET'S ROAD

Wine and woman and song,
Three things garnish our way:
Yet is day over long.

Lest we do our youth wrong,
Gather them while we may,
Wine and woman and song.

Three things render us strong,
Vine leaves, kisses and bay;
Yet is day over long.

Unto us they belong,
Us the bitter and gay,
Wine and woman and song.

We, as we pass along,
Are sad that they will not stay;
Yet is day over long.

Fruits and flowers among,
What is better than they:
Wine and woman and song?
Yet is day over long. [p. 110]

I will conclude this chapter with the words of Victor Plarr, whose little book on Dowson has served Dowson's memory more than he can have envisaged, certainly more than the scathing reviewers of 1914 would have credited:

> Yet Dowson's poetry has a kind of kinship to a certain sort of music, though he used to quote with amusement Gautier's dictum that music is the most disagreeable of sounds. His lovely poems that spring out so suddenly and inevitably among the classicisms, the verbiage, the prose poetry and futurist experiments of others, can truly be compared to some melody by some great composer who forgot for the nonce to be a great composer, as did the dying Schubert when he perhaps wrote the score of that sublime and longing lyric that is the theme of his 'Unfinished Symphony' . . .[22]

REFERENCES

1 Dr Mark Longaker, *Ernest Dowson* (Philadelphia, 1945), pp. 24 and 13.
2 W. R. Thomas, 'Ernest Dowson at Oxford', *The Nineteenth Century*, April, 1928.
3 Longaker, pp. 35, 36.
4 Longaker, pp, 35, 36.
5 Longaker, pp. 23, 54.
6 Longaker, pp. 23, 54.
7 Plarr, p. 14.
8 Plarr, pp. 13–14.
9 Plarr, p. 17.
10 Plarr, p. 30.

[11] 'A Note Upon the Practice and Theory of Verse at the Present Time Obtaining in France', *The Century Guild Hobby Horse* (London, April, 1891).

[12] *The Stories of Ernest Dowson*, ed. Longaker (London, 1946), p. 125.

[13] 'Ernest Dowson: An Interpretation', *The Catholic World* (New York, November, 1914).

[14] Plarr, p. 57.

[15] Geoffrey Tillotson, *Essays in Criticism and Research* (Cambridge, England, 1942), pp. 153 and 155. T. S. Eliot, in a preface to *John Davidson: A Selection of His Poems*, ed. Lindsay (London, 1961), confirms this view. He says that in the 'Cynara' poem, Dowson freed himself completely from the poetic diction of English verse of his time 'by a slight shift of rhythm.'

[16] All quotations from Dowson's poetry in this chapter are from *The Poems of Ernest Dowson*, ed. Longaker (Philadelphia, 1962).

[17] Plarr, p. 120.

[18] Jepson, *Memories of a Victorian*, p. 248. Dowson borrowed this from a source unknown to me and to Dowson. See *The Letters of Ernest Dowson*, p. 50.

[19] *Op. cit.*, p. 114.

[20] *The Times*, 27 June, 1896, p. 18.

[21] Introduction to *Poetical Works of Lionel Johnson* (London, 1915).

[22] Plarr, p. 65.

CHAPTER VIII

Lionel Johnson

AT the age of sixteen and a half, Lionel Johnson wrote from Winchester College to Francis Russell (later 2nd Earl Russell) who anonymously edited the letters from which I quote:

College,
October 7, 1883.

... I have not the smallest wish to go into the Church; but my choice of a career is limited to that and literature; to tell you the truth, I should like to burst upon the astonished world as a poet; there you have the height of my ambition. Somewhat conceited, is it not? but the amount of poetry, if I may use the word, that I have already perpetrated, would fill a respectable volume. I should like to turn out a kind of Matthew Arnold in a more professedly 'religious' way; i.e., combine the position of a man of letters with that of a quasi-religious lecturer. The only reason I should have for taking Orders would be the intense desire of getting hold of some of the rotten old pulpits occupied by dotards and exploding some more sensible and higher doctrines than any I have yet heard; but the explosion might bring the Church down about my ears. People of a certain class might accept from a 'priest' teaching they would reject from a layman. Still, I never really think the Church will be my destination.

Why do people want dogmas, and refuse to live without abstruse creeds? and why do they want to know everything, when they are quite as happy in reverent ignorance? I never felt the want of definite creeds, or of an anthropomorphic Saviour; I don't understand the need of them. If you want a powerful

> anti-clerical defence of the Godhead of Jesus, read Browning's 'Christmas Eve and Easter Day'; it is quite plain, and very powerfully put; the best thing about it being, that it leaves you to think what you like, without inflicting Church doctrine upon you . . .[1]

This letter, the first in the collection referred to, is as representative as any. Johnson never really changed his point of view. He did indeed, in later life, 'combine the position of a man of letters with that of a quasi-religious lecturer'—that was precisely the role which he was to fulfil for the remainder of his days. Reading the letters we observe his constant demand for some form of transcendentalism—does it matter what form it takes? To Johnson, of course, it did seem to matter. His reverence for Arnold influenced his thought and his verse permanently. But his desire to be 'a kind of Matthew Arnold in a more professedly "religious" way' betrayed his separateness from Arnold. With Arnold, culture, as T. S. Eliot has written, tended to usurp the place of religion. Johnson wished to put the religion back by means of what, copying Orwell's term, we may call 'double-think.' Far from reconciling Christianity with 'Aestheticism,' Johnson made one subserve the other according to his fancy or state of mind at the time. This conflict, leading as it did to moral tensions, appeared in his personal poems such as 'Dark Angel'; it explained the contrast between, say, 'A Dream of Youth' and 'Dominica in Palmis,' and was most explicit, perhaps, in 'To a Passionist':

Clad in a vestment wrought with passion-flowers;
Celebrant of one Passion; called by name
Passionist: is thy world, one world with ours?
Thine, a like heart? Thy very soul, the same?

Thou pleadest an eternal sorrow: we
Praise the still changing beauty of this earth.
Passionate good and evil, thou dost see:
Our eyes behold the dreams of death and birth.

We love the joys of men: we love the dawn,
Red with the sun, and with the pure dew pearled.
Thy stern soul feels, after the sun withdrawn,
How much pain goes to perfecting the world.

Canst thou be right? Is thine the very truth?
Stands then our life in so forlorn a state?
Nay, but thou wrongest us: thou wrong'st our youth,
Who dost our happiness compassionate.

And yet! and yet! O royal Calvary!
Whence divine sorrow triumphed through years past:
Could ages bow before mere memory?
Those passion-flowers must blossom, to the last.

Purple they bloom, the splendour of a King:
Crimson they bleed, the sacrament of Death:
About our thrones and pleasaunces they cling,
Where guilty eyes read, what each blossom saith.[2]

'Men of Assisi' considered two of her sons, representing the pagan-Christian conflict, Propertius and St. Francis. The same device was used in 'Men of Aquino' where Juvenal and St. Thomas are compared. 'Lucretius' considered singly the predicament of the good pagan.

Johnson's Christianity, if it may so be called, was a tenuous identification of subjective aesthetic responses and transcendental yearnings with orthodox Christian belief. His religion was (as Herbert Read said, I think rather meaninglessly, of Wordsworth's poetry) 'an extension of his personal psychology.' Johnson made God in his own image. I do not mean that he did not know the Christian dogma: indeed, he read constantly a great number of Christian works, from the Fathers of the Church to the preachers of his own day. But this declaration was typical:

> There is no hell: no sin: no anthropomorphism: no evil: no uncleanness: all love: no philosophy except of the spirit: I am a priest.[3]

Johnson was in love with what he took to be the beauty of holiness, with the old buildings of Winchester and Oxford and the traditions which they enshrine. In spite of his awareness of contemporary literature his own was essentially 'backward-looking'—his world that of Collins and Gray. Having already produced a considerable body of verse while at Winchester, he went on to give of his best during his years at Oxford and his early years in London. 'Winchester,' 'In Falmouth Harbour,' 'By The Statue of King Charles at Charing Cross,' 'Gwynedd,' 'Mystic and Cavalier,' 'Bagley Wood,' 'Trentals,' 'Sertorius,' 'Oxford Nights' were some of the fruits of his university years. These, together with criticism which he already contributed to some London journals, a second class in Classical 'Mods.' and a first class in 'Greats' were a rich and early harvest.

George Santayana was another friend of Russell's and, in a letter to him before his arrival at Oxford, Russell described some of those to whom he was introducing him:

> . . . [Jepson] is a funny fellow of immoral tendencies and pessimistic affectation. Well worth your visit to make him show off.
>
> [Johnson] is the man I most admire and—in the world, knows every book that is, transcendentalist, genius, and is called affected. The way for you to treat him is to take no notice when he tries (as he will) to shock you. If he discourses, listen: it will be worth while. . . .[4]

Santayana visited the two men and recounted his impressions:

> . . . I found [Jepson] in comfortable not very academic lodgings; the best available no doubt, yet hardly worthy of his ornamental person. He was not really good-looking, but his hair was yellow, parted in the middle and carefully waved, like a ploughed field. He said his life was devoted to the culture of it. Incidentally, however, he had accomplished a greater thing. He had already, at twenty, doubled human knowledge in one of the sciences, the science *de modis veneris*. There had been forty modes before, now there were eighty. . . . I was sceptical, and Jepson didn't interest me.[5]

He remarked concerning Johnson:

> Nor was he a philosopher, enduring the truth. He was a spiritual rebel, a spiritual waif who couldn't endure the truth, but demanded a lovelier fiction to revel in, invented or accepted it, and called it revelation. . . .[6]
>
> . . . he was a transcendentalist & a humanist; for that reason he seemed a prophet to Russell; and at bottom nothing could be more contrary to Christian humility and to Catholic discipline.

A religion of aestheticism such as, in effect, Johnson's was, could hardly develop with the years. His astonishingly youthful appearance, which he retained for most of his life, resembling, at Oxford—as Santayana wrote—'the head boy of a Preparatory School,' corresponded to a kind of stasis within. He was always to go on being that Winchester schoolboy, only becoming increasingly learned, increasingly adept at the skills of criticism, sending out a great patchwork of reviews and essays on the literary topics of the day. His early years in London appear from his letters to have been stimulating and enjoyable. On leaving Oxford in 1890 he moved, as has been related, into the 'Fitzroy settlement,' 20, Fitzroy Street, where lived Arthur Mackmurdo, Herbert Horne, Selwyn Image, and others; an ideal arrangement for him one would think. Nevertheless, winter in London was oppressive. In a letter dated 5 February, 1891, he wrote to his friend Campbell Dodgson:

> . . . But I have been in the depths of misery all through this weary autumn and insufferable winter. To begin with, the venomous fogs have nearly blinded me, and oculists have tortured me to death. I may have to go to a man at Lausanne in the Spring. Since I saw you in Oxford I have only been two weeks away from town: at Christmas, when I had to go home, and see my brother, before going out again to Burmah. He sailed on the first and has sent me two thousand cigarettes from Cairo on his way. Galton[7] is leaving me for good: London made him horribly ill:

and there were little incompatibilities of temper between him and Horne. They are both dear things and absolutely obstinate. Galton intends to take a desolate cottage on a Westmorland moor, miles from anywhere. We are looking out for a successor to him: won't you come? I have been getting a fair amount of work lately: especially for the new 'Anti-Jacobin', . . .

After describing a quite prodigious amount of journalistic work, Johnson continued:

. . . It sounds like flourishing business, but it isn't enough to live upon: and I am desperately worried by Oxford duns . . .
. . . I have lately seen a good deal of George Meredith, who is enchanting.
. . . We entertained the other night eighteen minor poets of our acquaintance: from Oscar Wilde to Walter Crane, with Arthur Symons and Willie Yeats between. They all inflicted their poems on each other . . .
. . . [Wilde] is publishing Dorian Gray as a book with additions which improve it: also a volume of essays, which, in ludicrous imitation of Pater, he calls 'Intentions'. I have made great friends with the original of Dorian: one John Gray, a youth in the Temple, aged thirty, with the face of fifteen . . .[8]

Johnson went on to describe Pater lecturing on Wordsworth at Toynbee Hall:

. . . he was ludicrously nervous. I met him at Aldgate, the station for Toynbee, half an hour before the lecture: so he said: 'Will you come and sit with me in some old city church till the time comes? I want to collect myself.' So we went and sat in solemn meditation in an ancient Wren church, very dark and smelling of . . . wood, like Oxford chapels. Oscar made a bon mot when Pater asked if he had heard him. 'Heard you? No! We overheard you': which was an admirable description. . . .[9]

In June, 1891, Johnson was received into the Roman Catholic Church by Father Lockhart who had been a friend of Newman's at Littlemore. Johnson was by then fully occupied with writing and lecturing and was a member of the Rhymers' Club.

In December, 1891, he wrote to Campbell Dodgson:

My dear Campbell,

I am writing in my arm chair by the fire: I have an arm chair now, and live in it: so my delicate scripture will probably be more than commonly dark. Here I have been enlightening the world through the columns of some half dozen papers since October: very busy and rather ill: my doctor says grim things

> about spinal paralysis which [annoy/worry?][10] me: sed non ego credulus istis. I lately refused an invitation to go to Yokohama for a year, to recover health under cherry trees upon the lower slopes of Fusijama. Lucky, I didn't go: for Fusijama has been vomiting lava by the square mile. My chief new employments and recreations are of a catholic kind. I have turned lecturer in general to all the Catholic societies in London and the adjacent districts. Twice have I held forth to Irish audiences upon the Gordon riots, at the Dominicans in Hampstead and elsewhere: and I am becoming notorious in that capacity. Wild Protestants deny my statements and insult my person: and in calming a controversial mob I have few equals. Then I take classes in literature at a sort of Catholic Toynbee Hall over the water in Southwark: Tennyson and Dante. It is very pleasant and [homely?], and I enjoy it all. One of my very best and dearest friends, Dowson of Queen's, has become a Catholic: carissime, when will you?
>
> Before Christmas will be published a small book called 'The Book of the Rhymers' Club' by twelve minor poets: le Gallienne, Symons, Rhys, Todhunter, Yeats etc and myself: at Elkin Matthews. It will, I sincerely think, be a success. There are six things of mine of which you may know two. At last, by the sweat of my brow, I have paid all my debts: so next spring I shall publish my own poems . . .
>
> . . . I sup with Richard Hill on Saturday at the Rainbow in Fleet Street, the Johnson Club anniversary: I shall probably meet my secret enemy Mr. Gosse. The extent to which that amiable ass blackguards me all over London is almost incredible, 'Oh you're the man that Gosse hates so' is a common form of address from strangers upon introduction. . . .[11]

I do not know what led to the estrangement from Gosse. While still at Winchester, in 1885, Johnson had received encouragement and criticism from Gosse and had replied gratefully, taking unusual trouble to write legibly.[12] Gosse no doubt assisted him with introductions in London though Johnson had no lack of these, his fame having preceded him. Rhys wrote that, at one of Gosse's 'Sunday afternoons,' Gosse mistook Johnson for a child and '. . . asked him if he would not like to go and play in the garden.' (*Everyman Remembers*, p. 122). But, while this may have been the beginning of an estrangement, it is obviously no cause for Gosse's 'blackguarding' Johnson, if, indeed, he ever did so.

The ill-health mentioned in the letters was not improved by the drinking which was an accompaniment to the literary life. Both he and Dowson and many of the 'nineties writers and artists were so favourably disposed to the artificial that the artificial state of mind which man has it within his power to create by alcohol became an increasing necessity. Their actual consumption was perhaps no more than that of many 'drinking men' but their nervous systems were too delicately balanced for such vigorous excitement It would appear that Johnson was actually 'expelled' from 20, Fitzroy Street because of his addiction. Galton had moved, as we have seen, and Horne left soon after. Mackmurdo, it seems, felt that he could no longer risk the consequences of Johnson's behaviour. Mr. Ian Fletcher reproduces part of a letter from Johnson to Mackmurdo:

> My dear Mackmurdo,
>
> I am exceedingly distressed by your letter, though I fully recognize your just cause of complaint. But may I ask for a further trial, upon the condition that I take the pledge at once—which I should have done long ago—and that upon giving the least disturbance I go. Also, I promise to have no drink in my rooms but for friends. As long as it depends upon my own will, I am quite hopeless: but the pledge is different. I once took it temporarily, for a month, and kept it rigidly: and should have taken it for good and all, but for falling ill. If you will consent to this, it will be the greatest of many kindnesses. Of course, should you be willing to do this, the Frasers must be told. I can't tell you how sorry I should be to leave the house where I have lived for five years and had so many friends. Medically speaking, I am not hopelessly given up to drink: it is easy for me to abstain altogether, though very hard to be moderate. At home and elsewhere, where I am not my own master, I drink nothing: it will be quite as easy here with the pledge. I shall be leaving town fairly soon, which will be best for me. If you will give me this last chance, I and my people will be more indebted to you than I can say.[13]

This was in 1895, in September of which Johnson moved to 7, Gray's Inn Square. The terrible decline had taken place over a short period of about three years. Gone altogether, no doubt, were any ideas of the priesthood.

In the summer of 1892 Johnson had walked through the West Country, pondering his critical work on Thomas Hardy:

> . . . all June I walked through Dorset: All September I was at Cadgwith, near Mullion. . . .[14]

His hopes had still been high, as the same letter shows:

> . . . I have no reason to apprehend that I shall be the new Laureate: au contraire, I vaguely contemplate taking orders. . . .

His book, *The Art of Thomas Hardy*, appeared in 1894 and established his reputation, being well received by Hardy himself, who met and knew its writer. His style owed much to Pater, particularly in the length and elaborate punctuation of his sentences which sometimes extend to a page and a half. Johnson's relationship with Pater was a close one and it is, I think, not improper to call him his disciple. Oscar Wilde, of course, was another disciple. We have seen that Johnson and Wilde met during these years in London, but there is little reason for believing that they spent much time together. Wilde is reported to have joked about Johnson leaving the Café Royal 'to hail the first passing perambulator.' He respected what he deemed the deep classical scholarship of Johnson and was no doubt pleased with the Latin tribute to the creator of Dorian Gray:

IN HONOREM DORIANI CREATORISQUE EIUS

Benedictus sis, Oscare!
Qui me libro hoc dignare
Propter amicitias:
Modo modulans Romano
Laudes dignas Doriano,
Ago tibi gratias.

Juventutis hic formosa
Floret inter rosas rosa
Subito dum venit mors:
Ecce Homo! ecce Deus!
Si sic modo esset meus
Genius misericors!

Amat avidus amores
Miros, miros carpit flores
Saevus pulchritudine:
Quanto anima nigrescit,
Tanto facies splendescit,
Mendax, sed quam splendide!

Hic sunt poma Sodomorum;
Hic sunt corda vitiorum;
Et peccata dulcia.
In excelsis et infernis,
Tibi sit, qui tanta cernis,
Gloriarum gloria. [1891]

Johnson often said, according to Plarr, 'Respectability is the best policy!' Had he not observed this policy it appears that he might have shared the fate of Wilde. His poem 'A Dream of Youth' (1889), in *The Century Guild Hobby Horse*,[15] and his contributions along with Wilde's and Douglas's to *The Chameleon*, reveal his homosexual propensities.

In a sense, the Rhymers' Club contributed to Johnson's undoing; for it was common for casual meetings to take place at the Crown, in Charing Cross Road, where drinks were served until after midnight. Then Dowson, and some others would be invited to 'Fitzroy' and continue talking and drinking until morning.

In 1893, before moving to Gray's Inn, Johnson had made a trip to Ireland with W. B. Yeats, in order to lecture to the Young Ireland League and other societies related to the revival of Celtic literature. One of these lectures was printed in *Poetry and Ireland: Essays by W. B. Yeats and Lionel Johnson* which was published by Yeats's sister, Elizabeth, at her Cuala Press in Dundrum (1908). The following extract exemplifies the vigorous lecturing style of the whole.

> . . . Now, I heartily hate the cant of 'art for art's sake:' I have spent years, in trying to understand, what is meant by that imbecile phrase. Also, I have a healthy hatred of the West Briton heresy. Further, no Irishman living has a greater love, and a greater admiration, for the splendid poetry of Davis, Mangan, and their fellows. But I dislike coercion in literature: and it seems to me an uncritical dictation of the critics, when they tell a writer, that he or she is no true Irish poet, because he or she does not write rousing ballads, or half-humorous love songs, or rhetorical laments, or a mixture of historical and political verse; and because he or she takes exceeding pains, with his or her workmanship and art. [p. 21] [I reproduce the punctuation as given.]

There is a brief rubric introduction to Johnson's essay which may be by Elizabeth Yeats. It may serve as our last word on Johnson as a speaker:

> . . . Lionel Johnson was small but delicately made, and with great dignity of manner, and he spoke with so much music that what had been in another monotony, became nobility of style. His reading or speaking of poetry befitted his own particularly, that had from scholarship and from the loneliness and gravity of his mind an air of high lineage, but even poor verses were beautiful upon his lips. I think no man ever saw him angry or petulant, or till his infirmity had grown on him, shaken from his self possession, and it often seemed as if he played at life, as if it were an elaborate ritual that would soon be over. I am certain he had prevision of his end, and that he was himself that mystic and cavalier who sang: 'Go from me, I am one of those, who fall. . . .' [p. 19].

From the time of this Irish venture Johnson became increasingly 'Irish' in his poetry, writing 'Parnell,' 'Ninety-Eight,' and some of the other verses collected in *Ireland, With Other Poems: 1897*. To the year 1893 belonged the poem 'The Dark Angel.' I will give the first two verses here:

> *Dark Angel, with thine aching lust*
> *To rid the world of penitence:*
> *Malicious Angel, who still dost*
> *My soul such subtile violence!*
>
> *Because of thee, no thought, no thing,*
> *Abides for me undesecrate:*
> *Dark Angel, ever on the wing,*
> *Who never reachest me too late!*

The emergence of the latent conflicts in the poet, between aestheticism and Christianity and morality gave rise to some of the most striking poems of his entire work. One might say that the repressed youth of Winchester and Oxford had very little to write *about*. The inspiration was essentially bookish. That is not, of course, a condemnation or even a necessarily pejorative reflection but is an explanation of why much minor verse *is* minor verse. Johnson's 'personal' poetry is the more moving, then, because it is expressing such an internal conflict. Weygandt wrote that Johnson's verse had 'the dignity and sonorousness of Browne, the tenderness of Otway, the melancholy and evening light of Collins.'[16] But he also wrote:

> In body Lionel Johnson was never more than a child, and there is, I think, something of that hardness of heart and narrowness of sympathy which lack of knowledge of the world preserves in children.[17]

Of the Rhymers, Johnson seems to have possessed the most acute mind. It is in the choice of application of his powers that he seems fallible. I can see Mr. Ian Fletcher's point that there was no-one, in the 'nineties, able 'to make an intellectual situation of which the creative power might profitably avail itself.'[18] This was the major function which Arnold had believed that critics should fulfil. To propose Pater for the role, as one might, is to invite the question: Did he create an *intellectual* situation? With regard to Pater's disciple, Johnson, I agree with Mr. Fletcher when he says: 'With him an unco-ordinated mental curiosity usurps the place of "a conscience in intellectual matters." '[19] For example we may take Johnson's periodical pieces, collected in *Post Liminium*, which range from Boswell to Pater, from Parnell to Marie Bashkirtseff.[20] Such a range would be admirable if some kind of connection were discoverable between the various pieces or if some common pattern of experience enabled the illumination of one writer by another. But there is little or no connection.

One cannot say that Johnson influenced the world of letters in any major way by his criticism, as one can say, for example, of Arnold that he countered the eccentricity and insularity of the English genius, encouraging restraint; or, of T. S. Eliot, that he initiated a revaluation of writers by a careful analysis of the exact sense of their works and of the relation between the form and the content. Arnold had insisted that for true appreciation of art it is necessary 'to get one's self out of the way.' Art is not a substitute for life but a means to a fuller understanding of it. The Pateran Aesthetes obliterated the distinction between art and life:

> . . . They wanted life to be art—in other words, they wanted a life purged of all its coarse, vulgar, trivial elements. Accordingly they turned away in life from all its inartistic elements. Where the poet's primary impulse may be said to be a 'religious' one, the attempt to grapple with experience and to find order and significance in it, and his artistic impulse only secondary, a continuation of the same impulse—the desire to embody and transmit his vision—the aesthetes made a religion out of art. They inverted the order of the creative mind and relegated the dynamic 'religious' principle to the periphery, where it became immobilized and nullified.[21]

This attitude involved,

> . . . that relativity in religion and morals, that distillation of intellectual essences into tenuous sentiment—even the most intractably logical subject might be dissipated into pure feeling—so characteristic of all Pater's writing.[22]

In Johnson's poetry, the subjectivity of the poet is such that he often fails to communicate with the reader. The rhetoric is that of the closet drama which takes place within the solitary's skull—all excitement within but odd and disquieting, often merely dull, in the form in which it is communicated. As Santayana wrote, '. . . after reading him through you are aware of a great wind of passionate language, but not of what was said or of what it was all about . . .[23] . . . the absence of all foundations, of all concreteness, of all distinction between fiction and truth, makes his poetry indigestible.'[24]

The quality above all which makes some of his poems memorable is their music. They remind us of the importance which the Rhymers attached to reading verse aloud. We shall search in vain for compression, for the striking image or confrontation in his verse. At his best there is a rain-washed clarity of description and statement, often descending to the merely prosaic but, when successful, impressive in its neatness and grace. 'Dead' is, I think, a fine example of prosodic virtuosity and illustrates the qualities I have been describing:

In Merioneth, over the sad moor
Drives the rain, the cold wind blows:
Past the ruinous church door,
The poor procession without music goes.

Lonely she wandered out her hour, and died.
Now the mournful curlew cries
Over her, laid down beside
Death's lonely people: lightly down she lies.

In Merioneth, the wind lives and wails,
On from hill to lonely hill:
Down the loud, triumphant gales,
A spirit cries Be strong! *and cries* Be still!

It is interesting to read of Ezra Pound's introduction to the works of some of the Rhymers, in America:

In America ten or twelve years ago one read Fiona MacLeod, and Dowson, and Symons. One was guided by Mr. Mosher of Bangor. I think I first heard of Johnson in an odd sort of post-graduate course conducted by Dr. Weygandt. One was drunk with 'Celticism', and with Dowson's 'Cynara' and with one or two poems of Symons's 'Wanderers' and 'I am the torch she saith':

I am the flame of beauty
And I burn that all may see
Beauty.

J's poems were about the last to catch one's attention. Their appeal is not so much to the fluffy, unsorted imagination of adolescence as to more hardened passion and intellect of early middle-age . . .
. . . If Gautier had not written, J's work might even take its place in Weltliteratur, that it might stand for its clearness and neatness.[25]

I cannot help feeling, however, that in his enthusiasm for Imagism, Pound may often confuse mere emptiness with that plain recording of sensory impressions which was then his objective. He finds affinities with Imagism in Johnson's line: 'Clear lie the fields, and fade into blue air.'[26] The immediacy of impression *is* striking in this line. Pound rightly calls Johnson 'a traditionalist of traditionalists' and says:

> He would have been content always writing Latin, I think, but failing that, he set himself the task of bringing into English all that he could of the fineness of Latinity. He wrote an English that had grown out of Latin.

Pound goes on to say that at his worst Johnson sinks into a 'Miltonian quagmire'; Johnson's poems are in 'short, hard sentences.'

> The reality is that they are full of definite statement. For better or worse they are doctrinal and nearly always dogmatic. He had the blessed habit of knowing his own mind, and this was rare among writers of his decade.[27]

Pound was deceived, I think. The 'definite statement,' the apparent finality of doctrine and dogma, what are they but the mould of a classical style into which Johnson has cast an imagination by no means 'hardened' or sorted? And in this Johnson resembles Arnold, of whom Eliot has written:

> Arnold, it is true, gave something else: he produced a kind of illusion of precision and clarity; that is maintained these qualities as ideals of style.[28]

In his criticism, as in his poetry, Johnson strove for correctness. This correctness and reverence for tradition, imbibed from Pater, extended, as we have seen, to the meetings of the Rhymers' Club. Their seriousness and calm good manners, their quietness, were tokens of respect to the poets in whose footsteps these men hoped to follow, were the outward counterpart of that inward calm intensity, the steady burning of the 'hard gem-like flame.' The imagination was all, but it must be kept in balance by sanity and order. Johnson wrote:

> . . . This it is, that makes the proper distinction of Milton, and of Arnold in our own day; that they had the classical and laborious virtues of perfection in art, yet without detriment to their poetical liberty of imagination. And whilst I hold Shakespeare and Browning in my heart of hearts, I cannot hold them blameless about matters, in which Milton and Arnold have but little or no blame.[29]

Born in happier days Johnson might have lived to a serene age, fulfilling his chosen function. The ideals he cherished, however, took no account of times and seasons, of the new industrial society, of the increasing democratization of the people. With a little more humour and common humanity he might have effected some kind of compromise with the modern world. Perhaps it is to his refusal or inability to be aware of it that we owe his verse. But the classical virtues of wholeness, sanity, harmony were not only in the mind and were certainly not the perquisite of small communities of recluses. At best the 'nineties could produce excellent imitations—but the spirit of Johnson was in conflict, not in harmony—he was indeed 'the victim of his own inspiration.'

REFERENCES

[1] *Some Winchester Letters of Lionel Johnson* (London, 1919), p. 15. 'A' in the letters is the editor, Francis Russell.

[2] Quotations from Johnson's poetry in this chapter are from: *The Complete Poems of Lionel Johnson*, ed. Ian Fletcher (London, 1953).

[3] *Winchester Letters*, p. 94.

[4] George Santayana, *The Middle Span* (New York, 1945), p. 54.

[5] *Ibid.*

[6] *Ibid.*, p. 56.

[7] Arthur Galton was a Roman Catholic priest in his late thirties who was at Oxford as an undergraduate while Johnson was there.

[8] In January, 1892, Dowson wrote to Plarr: '. . . And the latest news—that Gray, of whom I am seeing a good deal just at present, pursues the *Star* for a libel asserting him to be "The original Dorian of that name". This will be droll . . .' (Plarr, p. 60).

[9] British Museum. Add. MS. 46363.

[10] Johnson's 'scripture' is indeed 'more than commonly dark.' My parentheses indicate doubtful words.

[11] British Museum. Add. MS. 46363.

[12] British Museum: Ashley B658, f. 150.

[13] British Museum. Add. MS. 46363.

[14] *Ibid.*

[15] Vol. V, October, 1890. The poem was toned down in later versions. See *The Complete Poems*, pp. 341–343.

[16] C. Weygandt, *Tuesdays at Ten* (Pennsylvania, 1928), p. 63.

[17] *Ibid.*, p. 72.

[18] Ian Fletcher, *The Complete Poems of Lionel Johnson*, p. xiii.

[19] *Ibid.*

[20] *Post Liminium: Essays and Critical Papers by Lionel Johnson*, ed. Whittemore (London, 1911).

[21] D. S. Savage, 'The Aestheticism of W. B. Yeats,' *Kenyon Review*, VII: 1 (Winter 1945), p. 115.

[22] Fletcher, p. xiii.

[23] Santayana, p. 60.

[24] *Ibid.*, p. 56.

[25] Ezra Pound's introduction to *Poetical Works of Lionel Johnson* (London, 1915).

[26] 'April' (1889).

[27] Op. cit.

[28] T. S. Eliot, *Selected Essays* (London, 1932), p. 433.

[29] 'A Note Upon the Practice and Theory of Verse at the present Time Obtaining in France,' *The Century Guild Hobby Horse* (April, 1891), p. 61.

CHAPTER IX

John Davidson

IN 1895, Yeats had written to the effect that the arts were, as he believed, 'about to take upon their shoulders the burdens that have fallen from the shoulders of priests';[1] the arts were to fill our thoughts with the essences of things. This concept of the arts as secular theology was not new, of course, though its implications had not been worked out in England as fully as in France.

While Yeats was beginning to see the artist as the inheritor of the role of priest, there was one other Rhymer, John Davidson, who was in the process of becoming a prophet. Priest and prophet seldom get on together. While one is concerned with the preservation of what is most sacred in tradition, the other would destroy the old to make way for the new. It is therefore not surprising that Davidson's relationships with the other Rhymers were sometimes strained; it is even remarkable that a poet so different in background, temperament and artistic aims should have been one of their number. Probably the explanation lies in the marked difference between the Davidson who arrived in London, ardent for the literary life and those who contributed to it, and the same man after several years of self-realization and adversity. Frank Harris is a notoriously unreliable *raconteur* but it seems improbable that he would have any reason for misreporting mere facts of a man's appearance and demeanour in this case. The Davidson of 1889, whom he described, was:

> ... a little below middle height, but strongly built with square shoulders and remarkably fine face and head: the features were almost classically regular, the eyes dark brown and large, the

> forehead high, the hair and moustache black. His manners were perfectly frank and natural: he met every one in the same unaffected kindly human way: I never saw a trace in him of snobbishness or incivility. Possibly a great man, I said to myself, certainly a man of genius, for simplicity of manner alone is in England almost a proof of extraordinary endowment. I soon noticed one little peculiarity in Davidson, his enunciation was exceptionally distinct: every word had its value to him, each syllable its weight.[2]

But when Harris met him again in 1903 or 1904:

> ... He had grown self-assertive, and at the same time had developed a certain bitterness of attitude which seemed out of tune with his kindly temperament and fair habit of mind....

Harris attributed the change to the small recognition which Davidson's poetry (and most other poetry) received from a public more interested in music halls and the circus, to a hostile press, poverty, and ill-health.[3]

Morley Roberts did not find the 'decadent' aspects of the Rhymers altogether to his taste. Of all the Rhymers he preferred John Davidson; describing the rest as 'so much less men than he' and as 'mostly foolish young fellows, occasionally stumbling into beauty and then going half crazy because they could not pursue it....'[4]

In the same magazine article, Roberts recalls meeting Davidson at the Rhymers' Club and hearing him read 'certainly the best piece given us that night' and adds,

> ... perhaps this, proved to me by its scanty and grudging reception, was the cause of the next news I heard of the Rhymers' Club, which was that immediately on our departure those left behind resolved themselves into a committee and passed a resolution that there should be no more members elected. It was to be a sacred and forbidden place of resort and consolation for pure poets. This was told me by Davidson, not without laughter.

Yeats portrays a Davidson at odds with what seemed to him the effeminate pedantry of the Rhymers, their lack of 'blood and guts'.[5] In his public appearances, Davidson liked to appear 'healthy, popular, and bustling.' and his attempt to introduce four Scotsmen to the Rhymers' Club was intended to let in what Morley Roberts also would doubtless have considered a breath of fresh air. At one time it would appear that Yeats met with Davidson's approval; for the latter, on meeting him at a restaurant, shook his hand and proclaimed that he had 'blood and guts.' On another occasion, however, when Yeats had 'praised Herbert Horne for his knowledge and taste [Davidson] burst out "if a man must be a connoisseur, let him be a connoisseur in women."

Ernest Rhys writes of Davidson that '. . . he refused to become an out-and-out member [of the Rhymers' Club], saying he did not care to be ranked as one of a coterie . . .,' and goes on to describe '. . . his angry pride fostered by want of recognition by the public. . . .' Rhys adds:

> . . . Also there is such a thing as artistic jealousy, and a touch of it, added perhaps to another touch of temperamental incompatibility, had given John Davidson a lurking dislike to some members of the club. Of these Yeats was his pet aversion. I remember meeting him [Davidson] one day, a year or two after the Rhymers' Club had ceased to function, and recalling one or two books of poems by its members which had lately gained some vogue, and among the rest mentioning Yeats' 'Secret Rose'. With that he turned upon me and said with an angry laugh: 'I hate the Irish nation'.[6]

Dowson was evidently inspired by Davidson's complaints to try to recruit men of a sufficiently 'vigorous' stamp. In a letter to Victor Plarr, dated January, 1892, he wrote:

> . . . The latest Rhymer is one Barlas, a charming poet and anarchist, who was lately run in for shooting the House of Commons. . . .[7]

The Rhymers soon lost track of him, however, and later the same year, Dowson wrote to Charles Sayle:

> . . . To search for Barlas is like the search after the Sangreal. . . .[8]

John Evelyn Barlas used the pseudonym 'Evelyn Douglas.' An article on his work by H. S. Salt appeared in *The Yellow Book* XI (pp. 80–90). Salt deplores the small extent to which Barlas is known. He wrote: 'He is, if ever poet was, a Greek in spirit, but he possesses also, in a high degree, the modern sense of brotherhood with all that lives. A fiery impatience of privilege, authority, commercialism, breathes through all his writings; and therefore, like all poets who have held these burning thoughts, he is lonely, a stranger, an exile, as it were, from some Hid Isle of Beauty, who has been stranded on savage shores. This marked characteristic, the isolation of a proud but loving heart, will not be overlooked by any careful student of the eight small volumes of verse published by Barlas between 1884 and 1893. [In a footnote, Salt says 'All of these books are more or less difficult to obtain. The British Museum has a complete set . . .'] The preface, by Salt, to *Selections from the Poems of John E. Barlas* (Elkin Mathews, 1925) informs us that Barlas was born in

Burma in 1860, educated at Merchant Taylor's and New College, Oxford, and that he was for a while assistant classical master at Chelmsford Grammar School. He became involved with the Social Democratic Foundation and with William Morris' 'Commonweal'. He demonstrated in Trafalgar Square on 'Bloody Sunday' in November 1886 when he experienced, in his own words, 'the pleasure of being batoned and floored.' Salt says that this was the origin of the malady which darkened the latter part of his life. Barlas died in Glasgow in 1914. George Meredith is reported (by Salt) to have said that Barlas 'takes high rank among the poets of his time,' and, somewhat ambivalently, that his poems are 'unmatched for nobility of sentiment, and the workmanship is adequate.' My own reading of Barlas inclines me to 'concur with the common reader' who has allowed him to fade into the oblivion from which he only briefly and with difficulty ever emerged. Barlas cried to his goddess Euterpe:

> To me thou has given the pangs, and the chaplet of bay-leaf withheld.[9]

The Rhymers' decision against the election of further members appears to have been precipitated by the visit of Davidson with four Scotsmen referred to by Yeats:

> . . . He brought all four upon the same evening, and one read out a poem upon the Life Boat, evidently intended for a recitation; another described how, when gold-digging in Australia, he had fought and knocked down another miner for doubting the rotundity of the earth; while of the remainder I can remember nothing except that they excelled in argument. He insisted upon their immediate election, and the Rhymers, through that complacency of good manners whereby educated Englishmen so often surprise me, obeyed, though secretly resolved never to meet again; and it cost me seven hours' work to get another meeting and vote the Scotsmen out. . . .[10]

Davidson had worked reluctantly as a schoolmaster until his early thirties and then came to London to make a living by his pen. He was not altogether without introductions; his friend John Nichol had gone into retirement there from his professorship of English literature at Glasgow University. Davidson met John Lane, publisher of the *Yellow Book*, and became a regular contributor. He appears to have made a satisfactory living for some years from his poems, from his 'society' novels, and from translations such as that of Montesquieu's *Persian Letters*. But he became increasingly impatient of any work in the nature of journalism as his Muse became more insistent; so he came to know hardship. He became obsessed with ideas of human perfectibility and strength such as he expresses in *Mammon and His Message* (1908). There is a note of megalomania in such of his works. In his work while the Rhymers' Club was functioning we see the seeds from which his impatience with human feebleness and his belief in the Imagination proceeded. These poems, in their successful accommodation of urban and industrial images and their achievement of a colloquial idiom, were an inspiration to T. S. Eliot, who acknowledged his obligation to Davidson both for his own achievements in this direction and for technical hints, the latter with regard, in particular, to Davidson's poem 'Thirty Bob a Week'; in this poem 'Davidson freed himself completely from the poetic diction of English verse of his time,' and, Eliot goes on: 'I have a fellow feeling with the poet who could look with a poet's eye on the Isle of Dogs and Milwall Dock.'[11]

'Thirty Bob a Week' is, of course, in Kipling's manner; Davidson has, however, hit upon a character who represents the dim world of the suburban poor—a man truly representative of the many unheroic, routine-conditioned souls who have not the obvious appeal of the soldier or seafarer. The speaker in the poem is not a mere working type; he emerges, as Eliot has said, as a memorable individual. A sample may suffice:

[verses 8 and 9]
I step into my heart and there I meet
A god-almighty devil singing small,
Who would like to shout and whistle in the street,
And squelch the passers flat against the wall;
If the world was a cake he had the power to take,
He would take it, ask for more, and eat it all.

And I meet a sort of simpleton beside,
The kind that life is always giving beans;
With thirty bob a week to keep a bride
He fell in love and married in his teens:
At thirty bob he stuck; but he knows it isn't luck:
He knows the seas are deeper than tureens. [p. 73]

The term 'spasmodic' has been applied to Davidson and he certainly may be classed with those poets more intent on their message than on its form, often doggedly writing on when the Muse of poetry is no longer present. Selection is essential to enjoyment of his work and although it would be useful if there were a complete collection for easy reference it is doubtful if such a work would meet with general acceptance. The selected edition referred to appears to me truly representative of most that is best in his entire work.

'The Fleet Street Eclogues' (1893), and 'A Ballad in Blank Verse of the Making of a Poet' appear, at first sight, to be mere Shakespearean pastiche—and in many parts, indeed, are—but there are passages, particularly in the latter, which stand out as striking adaptations of modern urban images to Renascence blank verse. Such is his description of his home town of Greenock:

. . . this grey town
That pipes the morning up before the lark
With shrieking steam, and from a hundred stalks
Lacquers the sooty sky; where hammers clang
On iron hulls, and cranes in harbours creak,
Rattle and swing, whole cargoes on their necks;
Where men sweat gold that others hoard or spend,
And lurk like vermin in their narrow streets:
This old grey town, this firth, the further strand
Spangled with hamlets, and the wooded steeps,
Whose rocky tops behind each other press,
Fantastically carved like antique helms
High-hung in heaven's cloudy armoury,
Is world enough for me. [pp. 67–68]

Davidson wrote a good deal about his ideas of what poetry should be. His *credo* concerning poetry in the 'modern' world is expressed in the following extract from *A Rosary:*

Poetry is not always an army on parade: sometimes it is an army coming back from the wars, epaulettes and pipeclay all gone, shoeless, ragged, wounded, starved, but with victory on its brows; for Poetry has been democratized. Nothing could prevent that. The songs are of the highways and the byways. The city slums and the deserted villages are haunted by sorrowful figures, men of power and endurance, feeding their melancholy not with heroic fable, the beauty of the moon, and the studious cloisters, but with the actual sight of the misery in which so many millions live. To this mood the vaunted sweetness and light of the ineffective apostle of culture are, like a faded rose in a charnel-house, a flash of moonshine on the Dead Sea. It is not now to the light that 'the passionate heart of the poet' will turn. The poet is in the street, the hospital. He intends the world to know it is out of joint. He will not let it alone. Democracy is here; and we have to go through with it. The newspaper is one of the most potent forces in moulding the character of contemporary poetry. Burns's eyes were open; Blake's, perhaps, for a time; and Wordsworth had profound insight into the true character of man and the world; but all the rest saw men as trees walking; Tennyson and Browning are Shakespearian. The

> prismatic cloud that Shakespeare hung out between poets and the world! It was the newspapers that brought about what may be called an order of pre-Shakespearianism. It was in the newspapers that Thomas Hood found the 'Song of the Shirt'—in its place the most important poem of the nineteenth-century; the 'woman in unwomanly rags plying her needle and thread' is the type of the world's misery. The 'Song of the Shirt' is the most terrible poem in the English language. Only a high heart and strong brain broken on the wheel of life, but master of its own pain and anguish, able to jest in the jaws of death, could have sung this song, of which every single stanza wrings the heart. Poetry passed by on the other side. It could not endure the woman in unwomanly rags. It hid its head like the fabled ostrich in some sand-bed of Arthurian legend, or took shelter in the paradoxical optimism of 'The Ring and the Book'. It is true William Morris stood by her when the priest and the Levite passed by. He stood by her side, he helped her; but he hardly saw her, nor could he show her as she is. 'Mother and Son', his greatest poem, and a very great poem, is a vision not of a woman, but of a deserted Titaness in London streets; there was a veil between him also and the world, although in another sense, with his elemental Sigurds, he is the truest of all pre-Shakespearians. But the woman in unwomanly rags, and all the insanity and iniquity of which she is the type, will now be sung. Poetry will concern itself with her and hers for some time to come. Not much of the harlot: she is at ease in Zion compared with actual woe. The offal of the world is being said in statistics, in prose fiction; it is besides going to be sung. There it is in the streets, the hospitals, the poor-houses, the prisons; it is a flood that surges about our feet, it rises breast-high, and it will be sung in all keys and voices. Poetry has other functions, other aims; but this also has become its province.[12]

Davidson's reference here to 'the vaunted sweetness and light of the ineffective apostle of culture' is obviously to Arnold and his followers: possibly he has the Rhymers in mind, for was not Pater their master? In any event, this illustrates his antagonism to their poetic aims as he conceived them. Of course, one may say that a rhetorical piece such as this is intent on emphasizing the importance of 'engaged' poetry (as it has since come to be called) and is not necessarily to be taken literally as a condemnation of the 'disengaged.' Indeed, he has admitted in conclusion, 'Poetry has other functions, other aims. . . .' Probably Davidson was at first tolerant of those other aims which the Rhymers pursued but became increasingly impatient of them as a sense of prophetic purpose filled him.

It would be quite wrong, however, to label Davidson as a 'democratic' poet. For all his claim that the subject of English poetry must for some time to come be abject poverty he is not interested in organized social reform such as Shaw, and the Fabian group sought to bring about. He described Socialism as 'the decadence of feudalism'[13] and appealed to the individual will of man. One may discover in his distrust of systems, and reforming movements and in his quest for a new heaven and a new earth a refraction of that evangelical christianity which fettered his childhood and from whose influence he was never wholly able to escape. In *Mammon and His Message*, Davidson's rebellion against the idea of any external authority reaches its zenith. Davidson is God:

I'll carve the world
In my own image, I, the first of men
To comprehend the greatness of mankind;
I'll melt the earth and cast it in my mould,
The form and beauty of the universe.[14]

The 'message' is of revolt against a mechanized world and asserts the value of the instincts of man rather than of the intellect, in this, foreshadowing D. H. Lawrence, whom Davidson came to meet later. Rhys wrote:

> All the while Davidson was comforting himself with the splendid conceit that he was the greatest poet of his time. One day, when I asked him what he was doing in the British Museum reading room, he said: 'I've just finished the finest book that has been written for a thousand years!'[15]

On another occasion he met Davidson on Victoria Station and asked him what he had been writing. The poet replied, 'I write for three people, Dante, Shakespeare, and Jesus Christ.'[16]

Davidson, like Shaw, denied that his theories of the supremacy of man's will owed anything to Nietzsche. 'There are signs of a Nietzsche panic,' he wrote in the *Academy:*

> . . . and the word 'overman' is supposed to be an index of evolution in humanity. This seems to me very foolish. Nietzsche has nothing to tell the Englishman of the 'overman', the Englishman is the 'overman', in Europe, in Asia, in Africa, in America, he holds the world in the hollow of his hand. Moreover, he has been stated in our literature again and again, the instances being these: Marlowe's *Tamburlaine*, Shakespeare's *Richard III*, Milton's *Satan*, Carlyle's *Cromwell.*[17]

There is always a temptation to regard the writer who is 'engaged' with contemporary problems as performing a more vital task, as being more essentially 'alive' and in contact with the life around him. Sentimental 'values' are brought into conflict with purely artistic and critical ones. Prophecy, the invocation of sympathy for a particular depressed social class of a particular period, the exposition of philosophical ideas—these are laudable and valuable pursuits of man but are irrelevant to a consideration of poetry as poetry. Their incursion into art can only enforce a limitation of what should be of universal and timeless significance. Their admission is only artistically justifiable when they may be seen *sub specie aeternitatis*. 'The Song of a Shirt' may move almost unbearable pity in us but it is not a great poem because there is no universalization of its subject matter—it does nothing to its subject matter but present it in a graphic manner. In general one may say that a poem is vitiated to the extent that any propagandizing intent enters into it. The other Rhymers were concerned with what is eternal and essential in the life of man and with spiritual realities. Davidson's was, in my view, a more superficial intellect and emotionally off-balance perhaps as a result of his unhappy upbringing. Bernard Shaw, writing to Grant Richards in 1927, confirmed that Nietzsche had not influenced Davidson. 'His speciality was an attempt to raise modern materialism to the level of high poetry and eclipse Lucretius.' Shaw also gives reasons for Davidson's suicide. Davidson wanted to devote himself wholly to writing a great poem-drama that he had in his head but said he was unable to do so because it would earn him no money and he therefore had to drudge at journalism. Shaw asked him how long it would take him to write the play and how much he would usually earn from journalism in that time. He said six months and £250. 'I handed him £250, to be repaid out of half his royalties (if any) on the poem. He took the money, and gratefully resolved that he would enrich me for my generosity. So instead of writing the great poem he wrote what he thought would be a popular melodrama with millions in it. I believe I have a copy of this abortion somewhere.

When he realized that he had done me no good, and thrown away his chance, he killed himself. At all events that was the next I heard of him, poor fellow.

In short, he died of poverty. . . .'[18]

Lionel Johnson's condensed critique of the man and his work seems to me just:

> *Powerful* is the word: fervour, ardour, energy, rapid imagination and passion, sometimes heated and turbulent—a dash of Watson's sobriety would improve him. Intensely interested in *life* and its questions: a Scotch metaphysician turned into a romantic and realistic poet, without losing his *curiosity* about things. Versatile, experimentalist, prolific: writes ballads, which are psychological problems dramatically conceived and put,

with wonderful beauty of language at moments, but with a certain lack of delicacy—the poems rush and dash at you, overpower and invigorate you, rather than charm and enchant you. A restless poet—a true countryman of Burns and Carlyle, who has read the Elizabethans, and Keats and Browning. Earthy in a good sense; loves facts and Darwin: dreams and wonders and imagines, but always with a kind of robust consciousness. His beauty and his strength not in perfect accord. Take a poem of Watson; no amount of alteration would improve its decent and decorous mediocrity: Davidson's work often requires a last refining touch to transfigure it into a very wonderful thing. Hardest to estimate of all the younger poets: has tried so many ways and done so much. Has put genuine passion into his poetry, not an 'artistic' pose: full-blooded, generous, active: very human. Has not quite 'found himself' in literature or in life.[19]

REFERENCES

[1] *Essays and Introductions*, p. 193.

[2] Frank Harris, *Contemporary Portraits* (London, 1915), I, 120.

[3] *Ibid.*, p. 16.

[4] *John O'London's Weekly*, September, 1933.

[5] *Autobiographies*, p. 317.

[6] *Everyman Remembers*, p. 109.

[7] Reproduced in Plarr, p. 60.

[8] Letter reproduced in Longaker, p. 92.

[9] The interested reader may appreciate a list of Barlas' books: *Poems Lyrical & Dramatic* (Trübner & Co., Ludgate Hill, 1884); *Queen of the Hid Isle* (Trübner & Co., London, 1885); *Punchinello & his Wife Judith: a Tragedy* (A. Driver, Tindal St., Chelmsford, 1886); *Holy of Holies: Confessions of an Anarchist* (Printed by J. H. Clarke, High St., Chelmsford, 1887); *Phantasmagoria: Dream Fugues* (A. Driver, Chelmsford, 1887); *Bird-Notes* (Printed by J. H. Clarke, Chelmsford, 1887); *Love Sonnets* (Printed by J. H. Clarke, Chelmsford, 1889); *Songs of a Bayadere & Songs of a Troubadour* (Printed by James P. Mathew & Co., Cowgate, Dundee, 1893).

[10] *Autobiographies*, p. 391.

[11] Preface to *John Davidson: A Selection of His Poems*, ed. Maurice Lindsay (London, 1961), p. xi. Quotations from Davidson in this chapter are from this edition.

[12] Quoted by 'Hugh MacDiarmid,' in the Davidson edition referred to above, p. 53.

[13] Epilogue to *Mammon and His Message*, quoted by Lindsay, p. 34.

[14] *Mammon and His Message*, pp. 173–174.

[15] Rhys, *Everyman Remembers*, p. 91.

[16] Rhys, p. 91.

[17] Quoted by C. Weygandt, *The Time of Yeats* (New York, 1937), p. 57.

[18] Richards, *Author Hunting*, p. 224.

[19] Quoted by Ezra Pound in his introduction to *Poetical Works of Lionel Johnson*, p. xii.

CHAPTER X

The Dispersal of the Rhymers: Retrospect

THE disintegration of the Rhymers' Club and the end of the Decadent movement in England are parts of the same story. The Club's survivors were sufficiently cohesive to be still termed Rhymers for a while but they moved on to new circles of 'Georgians' or of 'Imagists,' maturing from a creative adolescence of which some of them appear to have become a little ashamed.

Dowson's *Verses* (1896) and the second edition of Symons' *London Nights* (1897) may be taken as marking the end of the Decadent movement in England.[1] Jepson gives interesting explanations of 'the end of the 'nineties.' He dismisses the notion that Wilde's conviction was the cause:

> . . . the truth is the 'nineties came to an end because the poets and artists were tired. In '97 Dowson and Beardsley were very tired and so was Lionel Johnson; they had done their best work. Conder and Whistler and Arthur Symons, the poet, had done their best work; Mr. Yeats had wandered off into the Celtic twilight.[2]

I think there is truth both in the conventional notion of Wilde's conviction representing a death-blow to the 'Aesthetic' movement *and* in the account of tiredness which Jepson gives. Tiredness, illness and death removed many of those mentioned: the reaction against Decadence affected the hardier remnant.

Already, in 1896, Dowson was battling against tuberculosis, moving from Paris to Brittany, finding his chief joy in work. He wrote, to Henry Davray from Brittany:

[The letter-card is post-marked 7. 6. 96.]

Hotel Gloanec, Pont Aven.

My dear Friend, Many thanks for your long and charming letter. I will write at greater length shortly. For the moment I am very busy & this is but a line to commend my book of 'Verses' to you, which Smithers will have sent you before now. I have had very nice letters about it from Symons, etc; both he and Yeats are to write about it but have had no reviews yet. I shall be very glad and flattered if you care to make me one of your series in *L'Hermitage*,—as I said before in a letter which I think may not have reached you, I shall be glad to give you any 'documents' you may require. Pierre Louÿs has sent me 'Aphrodite', & I am writing upon it for the next 'Savoy', also upon Tinan's 'Erythrée', which—*entre nous*—I do not much appreciate. *Aphrodite* is superb! I am in wretched health, with continual blood-spitting (alas! that Lebaudy is dead, & I cannot sell my *crachats*) but am doing much work, verse especially. Mes compliments à Madame Jeanne, Rambosson et *Cie*.

Tout votre

Ernest Dowson.[3]

From this, as from most of the letters which I have seen, one catches a glimpse of what Plarr called 'a Dowson *intime*':

> ... There were certainly two Dowsons—one the vexed and torn spirit of the biographers, the other a Dowson *intime*, known I venture to think to very few, but by those few greatly loved.[4]

The 'vexed and torn spirit' is portrayed in his last days by Rhys:

> ... On the last Rhymers' Club night he attended, he came late, and broke three long clays in succession in trying to light up. Then, asked if he had any rhyme to read, he pulled one out of his pocket, looked at it, shook his head, as much as to say it wouldn't do, and thrust it back again. . . .
> ... After that last visit to the Rhymers' Club he was not to be seen at any of his familiar haunts in Soho or Fleet Street. My last glimpse of him was on the steps of the British Museum. He looked three shades further gone in ill-health; his clothes were dusty, and a small red stain of blood on his collar emphasized the pallor of his face. Within a month or two more he was dead, and one of the Rhymers, Arthur Symons, was almost his last visitor.[5]

Dowson died at the home of R. H. Sherard in February, 1900.

By 1897 Johnson's plight was, it seems, worse even than Dowson's. George Santayana wrote:

> ... My last glimpse of him was in the summer of 1897, in Russell's rooms in Temple Gardens. It was a tragic spectacle. He still looked very young, though he was thirty, but pale, haggard, and trembling. He stood by the fireplace, with a tall glass of whiskey and soda at his elbow, and talked wildly of persecution. The police, he said, were after him everywhere. Detectives who pretended to be friends of his friend Murphy or of his friend MacLaughlin had to be defied. Without a signed letter of introduction he could trust nobody. He had perpetually to sport his oak. As he spoke, he quivered with excitement, hatred, and imagined terrors. He seemed to be living in a dream; and when at last he found his glass empty, it was with uncertainty that his hat sat on his head as with sudden determination he made for the door, and left us without saying good night.[6]

The accounts of Johnson's death in October, 1902, vary and the exact physical circumstances are, in any event, not highly important. He was, of course, well-connected socially and it would appear that much was done by relatives and friends to conceal the untidiness of his private life in order to preserve untarnished the public image of a scholar-divine. Arthur Waugh wrote:

> ... the truth was that sitting a-top of a high stool at the buffet of the Green Dragon in Fleet Street, he inadvertently overbalanced and fell on the back of his head. He had fallen on a deep Turkey carpet and no serious hurt seemed probable, but as he remained unconscious he was taken to Charing Cross Hospital.[7]

This does not agree with the *Daily Mail* account of 6 October, 1902:

> The many friends of Mr. Lionel Johnson, poet and critic, will learn with the deepest regret that he died on Saturday in St. Bartholomew's Hospital, having been found by a policeman unconscious in Fleet-street on Monday last. Throughout the week he has lain between life and death, with only a brief recovery of consciousness. . . .

Mrs. Carnegy Johnson wrote:

> ... The poor thing was ill when he removed from Lincoln's Inn to Clifford's Inn in March 1901 and apparently never could raise the energy for the very serious task of arranging all his books in his new quarters, nor was inclined to have a man in to do it for him. . . .

> . . . He was taken ill in Fleet St. with an apoplectic seizure about 10 o'C. on Monday night Sept. 29 & in his fall, fractured his skull: he was taken to St. Bartholomew's Hospital & never recovered consciousness till he died 2 a.m. on the Saturday. . . .[8]

Finally, the inquest proceedings (used in the introduction to *Complete Poems*, ed. Ian Fletcher) make it clear that Johnson died in the 'Green Dragon', as Waugh said. He fell trying to reach a chair and the main cause of death was a stroke.

In the *Daily Mail's* obituary notice, Boer War sentiment dictates the choice of extract, not a happy one, I feel, by poetic standards. I hope the reader will not object to the inclusion of the grotesquerie into which this article sinks at its close.

> . . . His verse was marked by an earnestness and austerity which recall his own beloved Lucretius. Not the least beautiful of his too occasional poems was his ode to the two Ferrands, brothers and intimate friends, who both fell gloriously for the national cause in South Africa. The pathetic lines—
>
> *You wait; I wait; a little while we wait;*
> *And then the wide flung gate,*
>
> have swiftly been fulfilled.
>
> Not the least strange fact in connection with this story is that Mr. Johnson was at one time the occupier of the haunted rooms, the curious phenomena in which were studied by two of the *Daily Mail's* correspondents in May of last year. It will be remembered that doors opened with no apparent reason, and that, the floor of the haunted room having been covered with powdered chalk, the prints of a bird-like claw were seen upon the chalk, though the observers had ascertained that the room was absolutely empty.
>
> It was stated to the inquirers who visited these rooms that previous occupants had died within a short period of leaving the rooms.[9]

The *Daily Chronicle* is less sensational, more genuinely obituary:

> . . . he took a first-class in 'Greats', and was rightly regarded by his contemporaries as one of the most brilliant scholars of his time. Coming to London, he soon became distinguished in the circle of young poets who formed the 'Rhymers' Club', but he published only two volumes of verse—'Poems' and 'Ireland, and Other Poems'. True poet as he was, it is perhaps by his critical work that he is best known. He possessed a depth and readiness of knowledge, an intuition of beauty, and an inspiring belief in the best intellectual things, only too rare in criticism . . . at the time of his accident he was engaged upon an article for the tenth

anniversary of Tennyson's death, which was to have appeared in our issue today. And now he is dead. As he sang in words so like Tennyson's, though written earlier:

> *I have passed over the rough sea,*
> *As over the white harbour bar.*[10]

The *Pall Mall*, of the same date said:

> . . . His monographs (on Mr. Hardy especially) and his occasional articles were full of insight and that fine literary balance which can only proceed from a calm and even estimate between the present and the past . . . there is lost to contemporary literature a true critic, corrective in his influence, ardent of spirit, and admirably sane in the tone and temper of his mind.

After reflection upon the tragic endings of Dowson, Johnson, and other poets at the end of the century, Yeats was unable to draw a firm conclusion as to their cause. He considers poverty but rejects this on the ground that Johnson had private means. He seems to have overlooked Davidson whose death *was* according to Shaw caused by poverty. I think that Yeats is nearest the truth when he attributes the tragedy to 'our form of lyric, our insistence upon emotion which has no relation to any public interest.' Yeats finds this conclusion weakened by his remembering that:

> the first to go out of his mind had no lyrical gift, and that we valued him mainly because he seemed a witty man of the world; and that a little later another who seemed, alike as man and writer, dull and formless, went out of his mind, first burning poems which I cannot believe would have proved him as the one man who saw them claims, a man of genius.[11]

Yet the fact that men without real talent (I am not clear to which specific persons he refers here) may have shared in the tragedy does not invalidate the argument, I think. Every 'movement' has its camp-followers, and it is not uncommon for these to go to extremer lengths than the leaders, their very lack of talent compelling them to make hysterical gestures of empathy as a substitute.

It should have appeared from this study that the stresses to which a Dowson, a Verlaine, or a Johnson (to cite only a few) were subject were an inevitable concomitant of that deification of the individual which followed a rejection of exterior moral compulsions. Johnson's or Dowson's Catholicism was rendered invalid as a saving force because it formed only a part of their world-view: it had to co-exist with their more vivid sense of the sacredness of an artistic inspiration owing little or nothing to received religion—centred in the self and its pristine reactions to phenomena. However melodramatic it may seem, it is right, I think, to view 'the tragic generation' as martyrs to 'a conscience in intellectual matters' in a country which had not been distinguished for that in its cultural, economic, or political life. The exaggeration of some of their gestures has to be viewed in the context of the Philistinism and industrial squalor of late Victorian times. The disorder of their lives reflects the moral chaos which underlay the sober and dignified forehead of the time. It is when we read their work that we recognize that note of individual candour and honest perception which the Victorian period had so often smothered in its fear of the abyss which 'free-thinking' had opened at its feet. Victorian thinkers had themselves undermined the ground upon which their society was based, but continued to behave as if nothing had fundamentally changed. 'Decadence' was an attempt of the imaginative spirit to come to terms with the damage.

Those Rhymers who survived the stressful years tended to become assimilated with the 'Georgian' writers or with the new group of Imagists of whom Ezra Pound was the progenitor and Amy Lowell the succouring mother. An interesting sketch of one aspect of the new society of poets, into which some of the surviving Rhymers entered for a time is given by Rhys. Yeats's presence, of course, does not indicate an affinity with either Georgians or Imagists and it will be as well to discard these group-terms and to consider the party assembled here as simply poets:

> At our house in Hermitage Lane—called 'Derwen' after the old oak tree staring in at the window—to which we had moved from Hunt Cottage, we often had gatherings of young poets, resuming the nights at the Old Cheshire Cheese of the Rhymers' Club. Many of the Rhymers came to these Derwen occasions; but we were allowed more rope in making up the lyric team, and usually asked some women writers to join the company.
>
> The most memorable of these nights was one when the late D. H. Lawrence, then a completely unknown poet, came with Ford Madox Ford (who was editing the *English Review*). He had written to say he had discovered a wonderful new poet in a young country schoolmaster somewhere in the Black Country, and wished to bring him along. . . .
>
> . . . When the two entered the room together, they made a strong contrast. Ford always had the air of a man-about-town used to town occasions, while Lawrence looked shy and countrified; perhaps a little overwhelmed by the fanfaron of fellow poets heard in the room, with W. B. Yeats and Ezra Pound dominating the chorus. . . .
>
> . . . During the supper, Yeats, always a good monologuer, held forth at length on this new way of bringing music and poetry together, and possibly Ezra Pound, who could also be vocal on

occasion, may have felt he was not getting a fair share of the fun. So, in order to pass the time perhaps, and seeing the supper table dressed with red tulips, he presently took one of the flowers and proceeded to munch it up. . . .

. . . The plan of entertainment on these occasions was a simple one. Every poet was supposed to bring an original poem and read or declaim it aloud. Willie Yeats was a capital opener of the feast, and that night we asked him, as he said he had no new verses to read, to recite *The Lake Isle of Innisfree;* but he said he was tired of that lovely lyric, and read us instead a later one which begins:

'She lived in storm and strife,
Her soul had such desire
For that proud death may bring . . .'

At that moment, a fresh arrival created a diversion . . . Hugh Law, M.P. . . . reminded us how wonderfully he [Yeats] had paraphrased Ronsard's sonnet:

'Quand vous serez bien vieille, au soir,
à la chandelle,
Assise auprès du feu, devidant et filant . . .'

Hugh Law recited the sonnet for us movingly, with perfect accent; and then he begged Yeats to give us his version, which, after explaining it was not a literal one, he proceeded to intone:

'When you are old and grey and full of sleep
And, nodding by the fire, take down this book,
And slowly read, and dream of the soft look
Your eyes had once, and of their shadows deep;
. . .

It ended:

'And bending down beside the glowing bars,
Murmur, a little sadly, how love fled
And paced upon the mountains overhead,
And hid his face amid a crowd of stars.'

But Hugh Law reminded us that Ronsard had ended it differently, and I suggested a closing couplet—after Yeats had gone (for I knew it would not pass the fastidious Yeatsian test):

'Regret then, in your dream, your proud disdain
And take my love and your lost youth again.'

> Ernest Radford . . . whose method was entirely unlike Yeats's, but admirable as a foil, read us two lyrics, one of which, quite enough to keep a man's memory alive, began:
>
> *'Oh what know they of harbours*
> *Who toss not on the sea'. . . .'*
>
> And that is how one likes to remember him, in his prime, before the sad decay of his wonderful brain.[12]

Rhys goes on to describe D. H. Lawrence reading:

> *Whativer brings thee out so far*
> *In a' this depth o' snow. . . .*

and continuing for over half-an-hour so that the hostess had to intervene. After this Ezra Pound, sounding a little, Rhys says, like Henry Irving with an American accent declaimed his *Ballet of the Goodly Fere*. There was some objection to the word 'fere' but it was generally agreed that a poet had a right to make his own dialect. Rhys continues:

> Unexpectedly John Davidson came—very late, and refused point-blank to contribute his quota. However, after some persuasion, he read us his 'In Romney Marsh' which had a great ring in it, lines only Davidson could have written. . . .

In 1909, John Davidson walked into the sea off Land's End—not to return. He who had stressed above all the importance of the individual will believed also in every man's right to end an insupportable life.

In 1919, Arthur Waugh looked back upon the years of the Rhymers' Club:

> The surrounding movement was essentially one of emancipation. There were Celtic poets in the coterie, and Cymric poets, and poets of the London streets, and celebrants of the naked passions; but among all of them the dominant impulse was a determination to stir poetry out of the rut into which the crowd of Tennysonian euphuists had driven it. The rapt visionary on the one hand, and the eager realist upon the other, were at least united in this. The dust of ages had to be beaten out of the bookshelves: a new sincerity was to make all things plain. tradition must be broken with, and the contemporary world interpreted in the light of some burning new idea. . . . Lionel Johnson, on the contrary, felt no need for new ideas: for him 'the old was still the true.' Turning back to the still honoured classics, he was content to draw from them all the inspiration that he needed for his contemplative and contented life. . . .[13]

In an article in the *Daily Chronicle*, Arthur Waugh had previously made the appearance of Le Gallienne's *New Poems* (London, 1910), the occasion for a lengthier retrospective view:

> A new volume of poems by Mr. Richard Le Gallienne bearing the imprint of *The Bodley Head*, comes like a faint but haunting echo from the days when we were all younger. Is it really fifteen years since the Rhymers' Club was broken up? And who remembers their melodies now? Mr. Yeats has fled to Ireland—a country from which he only issued, as it were, a changeling—but what should Mr. Le Gallienne do in America? Fifteen years ago he could scarcely have imagined a less congenial soil. How should he sing the Lord's song in a strange land? Mr. Ernest Rhys is busy editing learned classics for the million [the 'Everyman' series], and only too seldom strings his Celtic lyre to music. Mr. Arthur Symons is unhappily ill. The deaths of Lionel Johnson and Ernest Dowson are bitterly fresh in the memory. All the little company is scattered, and Mr. Le Gallienne's reappearance from under the old Bodley bust seems like some strange survival of forgotten associations. No reviewer of sensibility who remembers the age of the Rhymers and the youth of *The Yellow Book* will open this inviting volume without a touch of sentiment. Of course, they had their weaknesses and affectations, these Rhymers of our youth. They were none of them above riding their Pegasus through the public streets, and some even assumed a Viking air of conquest in flowing locks and wide gesticulations. But, after all, they did care. They did care very much for poetry, and there was something infectious about their enthusiasm, for they made other people care as well. 'Publishers and sinners', as Mr. Nevinson likes to call them, were not afraid to look at verse in those days; literary editors were not sparing of space for their reviewing. In those days page three of the *Daily Chronicle* glittered every week with the discovery of genius. Does anyone care so much for poetry now?[14]

Although, as we have seen, the Rhymers' Club brought together men of appreciably diverse attitudes, W. B. Yeats, in his recollections of the group, always tends to think above all of Johnson and Dowson and of the Decadence. He admitted this after a lecture in which he had overlooked many other Rhymers who were still alive. Rhys, one of these, had remonstrated and called forth a letter from which I quote:

> . . . For the moment I forgot both Plarr and you in my pleasure at the thought that Greene had showed so much genius—a sort of fat weed on Lethe's wharf; then re-wrote the sentence to bring in Plarr who had done a little beautiful work—nature is so

miserably incomplete and so little respects our sentences. Neither you nor Rolleston came into my head at the moment. One begins to think of 'The Rhymers' as those who sang of wine and women—I no more than you am typical.[15]

The tendency to remember, above all, those 'who sang of wine and women' persisted, as Yeats's BBC broadcast in 1938 illustrated:

... In those days I was a convinced ascetic yet I envied Dowson his dissipated life. I thought it must be easy to think like Chaucer when you lived among those morbid, elegant, tragic women suggested by Dowson's poetry, painted and drawn by his friends Conder and Beardsley. You must all know those famous lines that are in so many anthologies:

Wine and women and song,
To us they belong,
To us the bitter and gay. ...[16]

Yeats went on to describe some of Dowson's dissipations and debaucheries (largely, as we have seen Gawsworth and Dr. Goldfarb complain, reported from hearsay) and Johnson's untruths and alcoholism. Curiously, in Yeats's memory of the Rhymers, Ernest Dowson alone seems to subsume *all* of the others; for Johnson really did not sing 'of wine and women' and certainly in real life preferred whisky and solitude.

And in the poem 'The Grey Rock' in which Yeats celebrates the:

Poets with whom I learned my trade,
Companions of the Cheshire Cheese ...

Dowson and Johnson take pride of place:

... You had to face your ends when young—
'Twas wine and women, or some curse—
But never made a poorer song
That you might have a heavier purse,
Nor gave loud service to a cause
That you might have a troop of friends.
You kept the Muse's sterner laws,
And unrepenting faced your ends,
And therefore earned the right—and yet
Dowson and Johnson most I praise—
To troop with those the world's forgot,
And copy their proud steady gaze.[17]

My study has shown the inadequacy of Aestheticism alone as a guiding motive in some of the Rhymers' lives and, it must be added, in the creation of more than minor poetry. That the word 'minor' is not pejorative is surely understood. But Yeats did not intend to remain a minor poet and found his own highly personal solution to the dilemma of the absence in modern society of a meaningful collective 'myth.'

It is not uncommon to read derisive or denigratory comment on the Rhymers, dismissing them as dreaming failures. Their failure, such as it was, however, has taken great pains and much time for their successors in the craft of poetry to remedy. In this century we have the attempts of T. S. Eliot and of Ezra Pound to correlate the fragments of a spiritually shattered world and these attempts have received—at least in the case of Eliot—a just meed of applause. But it seems doubtful whether the bridging of the chasm between art and life has been made much more secure. It seems to me increasingly apparent that poetry will have no alternative, if it is to retain its integrity, but to become increasingly domestic and personal. As the possibility of the construction of a meaningful 'myth' within which to interpret modern life is seen more than ever to be chimerical, poets will content themselves with a faithful rendering of their individual successes in creating private, limitedly meaningful worlds.

REFERENCES

[1] An observation for which I am indebted to Professor Enid Starkie, *From Gautier to Eliot* (London, 1960).

[2] *Op. cit.*, p. 287.

[3] British Museum, Ashley B658, f. 150.

[4] Plarr, p. 9.

[5] Rhys, *Everyman Remembers*, p. 105.

[6] *The Middle Span*, p. 59.

[7] Arthur Waugh, *Memories* (London, 1924), p. 125.

[8] British Museum. Add. MS. 46363. A letter from Carnegy Johnson to Campbell Dodgson dated 17 October.

[9] The *Daily Mail*, 6 October, 1902.

[10] The *Daily Chronicle*, 6 October, 1902.

[11] *Autobiographies* (London, 1961), p. 300.

[12] *Everyman Remembers*, p. 251.

[13] Arthur Waugh, *Tradition and Change* (New York, 1919), p. 100.

[14] Quoted by J. Lewis May, *John Lane and the Nineties* (London, 1936), pp. 92–93.

[15] Reproduced, undated, in Ernest Rhys, *Letters from Limbo* (London, 1936), p. 158. The lecture is referred to in a letter from W. B. Yeats to his father, dated 16 February, 1910: '. . . a lecture I am to give in a private drawing-room in London next month. The lecture is on Contemporary Poetry, a vague name chosen before I knew what the lecture was going to be about. I am describing the group of poets that met at the Rhymers' Club, more especially Ernest Dowson. The doctrine of the group, or rather of the majority of it, was that lyric poetry should be personal. That a man should express his life & do this without shame or fear. Ernest Dowson did this & became a most extraordinary poet, one feels the

pressure of his life behind every line as if he were a character in a play of Shakespeare's. Johnson had no theories of any sort but came to do much the same through the example of Dowson & others & because his life grew gradually so tragic that it filled his thoughts. His theory was rather impersonality so far as he had any, I should say. In poetry the antithesis to personality is not so much will as an ever growing burden of noble attitudes & literary words. . . .' (*The Letters of W. B. Yeats*, ed. Wade, p. 547).

[16] W. B. Yeats, *Essays and Introductions* (London, 1961), pp. 492–493.

[17] *The Collected Poems of W. B. Yeats* (London, 1958), p. 115.

Appendix I

THE RHYMERS' CLUB

(Contributed by W. B. Yeats

to

The Boston Pilot, 23 April, 1892)

IN France literature divides itself into schools, movements and circles. At one moment the Decadents, at another the Symbolists, today the Parnassians, tomorrow the Naturalists, hold the public ear and win acceptance for their theory and practice of literature. In England the writers do not form groups, but each man works by himself and for himself, for England is the land of literary Ishmaels. It is only among the sociable Celtic nations that men draw nearer to each other when they want to think and dream and work. All this makes the existence of the Rhymers' Club the more remarkable a thing. Into this little body, as about a round table of rhyme, have gathered well nigh all the poets of the new generation who have public enough to get their works printed at the cost of the publisher, and some not less excellent, who cannot yet mount that first step of the ladder famewards. Not that the Rhymers' Club is a school of poets in the French sense, for the writers who belong to it resemble each other in but one thing: they all believe that the deluge of triolets and rondeaus has passed away, and that we must look once more upon the world with serious eyes and set to music—each according to his lights—the deep soul of humanity. 'What is the good of writing poetry at all now?' said the other day a noted verse writer whose fame was at its height ten years ago. 'Sonnets are played out and ballades and rondeaus are no longer novel, and nobody has invented a new form.' All, despairing, cry of the departing age, but the world still goes on, and the soul of man is ever young, and its song shall never come to an end. The names of some few of the Rhymers may have already been blown across the Atlantic, though more probably they have not, for all but one are of the very newest literary generation. There is Arthur Symons, who has made the music halls of London and Paris his peculiar study, and set forth their gaieties and tragedies in even, deftest verse, and John Davidson, who has just published a series of poems on a Scotch music hall. In both writers one finds that search for new subject matter, new emotions, which so clearly marks the reaction from that search for new forms merely, which distinguished the generation now going out. 'He is no poet who would not go to Japan for a new form,' wrote a distinguished member of the Gosse, Lang and Dobson school.

Athur Symons is a scholar in music halls as another man might be a Greek scholar or an authority on the age of Chaucer. He has studied them for purposes of literature and remained himself, if I understand him rightly, quite apart from their glitter and din. He has gone to travel among them as another man might go to travel in Persia, and has done it thoroughly, being familiar with those of many cities. John Davidson, upon the other hand, claims to have lived his verses. In the Prologue to his just published *In a Music Hall*, one reads:

I did as my desk-fellows did;
With a pipe and a tankard of beer,
In a music-hall, rancid and hot,
I lost my soul night after night.
It is better to lose one's soul,
Than never to stake it at all.

No two attitudes towards the world and literature could be more different, and despite the community of subject no two styles could be more dissimilar than those of John Davidson and Arthur Symons. One has more fire and enthusiasm, and the other more art and subtlety. Fine as much (notably the haunting and wonderful Selene Eden) certainly is, I find my enjoyment checked continually by some crudity of phrase. The din and glitter one feels were far too near the writer. He has not been able to cast them back in imaginative dimness and distance. Of Mr. Symons' method I will speak at length when his book comes to me. I have but seen stray poems and judge from them that, despite most manifest triumphs from time to time, he will sometimes fail through gaining too easily that very dimness and distance I have spoken of. He will, perhaps, prove to be too far from, as Mr. Davidson is too near to, his subject. I must say that the author of *In a Music Hall* is entirely successful in some of the romantic poems that follow the *Music Hall* verses. Notable is that radiant poem in which the gleeman tells how

Starry truth
Still maintains a changing strife
With the purple dreams of youth;

and notable also are For Lovers, and parts of Anselm and Bianca.

Both writers are, whether they succeed or fail, interesting signs of the times. Not merely are they examples of that desire for new subject matter of which I have spoken, but of the reaction from the super-refinement of much recent life and poetry. The cultivated man has begun a somewhat hectic search for the common pleasures of common men and for the rough accidents of life. The typical young poet of our day is an aesthete with a surfeit, searching sadly for his lost Philistinism, his heart full of an unsatisfied hunger for the commonplace. He is an Alastor tired of his woods and longing for beer and skittles.

The most like Alastor in appearance among the Rhymers is certainly Richard Le Gallienne. The Review of Reviews has made many familiar with his refined Shelley-like face, and his own *Book Bills of Narcissus*—a half romance, half autobiography—with his moods and his history. The longing for Philistine beer and skittles has perhaps beset him less ardently than the bulk of his fellows, and he still prides himself on wearing the ambrosial locks of the poet. The longing for a new subject has filled him as full as his neighbours, however, and has led him to publish a book of poems, *Volumes in Folio*, which has dealt with nothing in the world but the buying and treasuring of rare books. A very pleasant glamour of Keats-like romance did he weave about them, too. But *Volumes in Folio* is ancient history, and I have to do but with the present and the future. Lionel Johnson, who has somewhere about him a long poem called Gloria Mundi, full of Catholic theology, and George Greene, who is writing a whole book of verse on the *Inferno* of Dante, are other typical members. Ernest Rhys, of Camelot fame, and T. W. Rolleston are constant frequenters. I need not multiply names. They will all be on the title page of the forthcoming *Book of the Rhymers' Club*, the manifesto of the circle.

I said that all, with one exception, belong to the newest literary generation. That exception is important, for it is Dr. Todhunter, who has just published a shilling edition of his book of Irish poems, and so concerns us more than all the others. If we do not take care of our own singers, who will? The book is called *The Banshee* and is sold by Sealy, Bryers & Walker, Middle Abbey Street, Dublin. I need not say much now about it, for it was reviewed enthusiastically and fully by all the Irish-American papers on its first appearance a couple of years ago. In it Dr. Todhunter follows in the footsteps of Sir Samuel Ferguson and gives us simple and stately versions of The Children of Lir and Sons of Turann. There is no better way of getting a knowledge of two of the most lovely of all the old Irish stories than from this book. May many follow in the road Dr. Todhunter has chosen. It leads where there is no lack of subjects, for the literature of Ireland is still young, and on all sides of this road is Celtic tradition and Celtic passion crying for singers to give them voice. England is old and her poets must scrape up the crumbs of an almost finished banquet, but Ireland has still full tables.[1]

REFERENCES

[1] The article is reproduced in *Letters to the New Island*, ed. Horace Reynolds (Cambridge, Mass., 1934).

Appendix II

THE BOOK OF THE RHYMERS' CLUB: London, Elkin Mathews, At the sign of the Bodley Head, In Vigo Street, 1892.

Contents in order of their inclusion:

At the Rhymers' Club: The Toast	Ernest Rhys
What of the Darkness	Richard Le Gallienne
By the statue of King Charles the First at Charing Cross	Lionel Johnson
A man who dreamed of Fairyland	W. B. Yeats
Carmelite Nuns of the Perpetual Adoration	Ernest Dowson
Love and Death (Aesop's Fable)	Ernest Radford
Epitaphium Citharistriae	Victor Plarr
Beatrice's Song (From 'The Poison Flower')	John Todhunter
The Pathfinder	G. A. Greene
The Broken Tryst	Arthur Symons
New World and Old	E. J. Ellis
A Ring's Secret	T. W. Rolleston
The Wedding of Pale Bronwen	Rhys
Beauty accurst	Le Gallienne
O Mors! etc.	Dowson
The Sonnet	Greene
A Burden of Easter Vigil	Johnson
To One Beloved	Todhunter
Music and Memory	Symons
In a Norman Church	Plarr
Father Gilligan	Yeats
Amor Umbratilis	Dowson
At the Hearth	Ellis
Keats' Grove	Greene
On Marlowe	Rhys
At Citoyenne Tussaud's	Plarr

Ballade of the 'Cheshire Cheese'	Rolleston
The Last Music	Johnson
A Death in the Forest	Symons
'Onli Deathe'	Radford
Ad Domnulam Suam	Dowson
Dedication of Irish Tales	Yeats
Quatrain (The Epitaph on Hafiz, a young linnet)	Rhys
Javanese Dancers: A Silhouette	Symons
Chorus from 'Iphigeneia in Aulis'	Todhunter
To a Greek Gem	Plarr
Arts Lough	Greene
In Falmouth Harbour	Johnson
A Choice of Likenesses	Radford
To Autumn	Le Galienne
Vanitas	Dowson
A Fairy Song	Yeats
Mothers of Men	Ellis
Chatterton in Holborn	Rhys
To a Passionist	Johnson
Freedom in a Suburb	Radford
Quatrain: Les Bourgeoises	Rhys
Drifting	Greene
Villanelle of Sunset	Dowson
The Lake Isle of Innisfree	Yeats
A Sundial: Flowers of Time	Radford
Twilight-Piece	Plarr
Sunset in the City	Le Gallienne
An Epitaph	Yeats
Proverbs	Ellis
Plato in London	Johnson
The Song of the Songsmiths	Greene

THE SECOND BOOK OF THE RHYMERS' CLUB: London, Elkin Mathews and John Lane. New York: Dodd, Mead and Company, 1894.

Contents in order of their inclusion:

In Westminster Abbey: October 12, 1892	Todhunter
Beyond?	Greene
Ad Cinerarium	Plarr
Extreme Unction	Dowson
Solace (In Memoriam W. H. W.)	Radford
Lost	Radford
Mystic and Cavalier	Johnson

The Rose in My Heart	Yeats
Howell the Tall	Rhys
A Ballad of London	Le Gallienne
Venus	Ellis
Nora on the Pavement	Symons
Morning: Cycling Song	Rolleston
The Invasion of Brittany	Hillier
To a Breton Beggar	Plarr
Glories	Johnson
The Song of Tristram	Todhunter
To One in Bedlam	Dowson
Proserpine (For a Picture)	Greene
The Folk of the Air	Yeats
Song	Radford
Love's Exchange	Le Gallienne
In Excelsis	Hillier
Love and Art	Symons
A Year of the River	Ellis
Noon-day (Elegiacs)	Rolleston
Song of the Wulfshaw Larches	Rhys
To Morfydd	Johnson
Deer in Greenwich Park	Plarr
Non Sum Qualis etc.	Dowson
Euthanasia (fin de siècle)	Todhunter
'Violets Full'	Greene
The Second Crucifixion	Le Gallienne
The Fiddler of Dooney	Yeats
Orpheus in Covent Garden	Hillier
Song in the Labour Movement	Radford
Evening (Evensong)	Rolleston
Peace	Ellis
Song	Symons
Death and the Player	Plarr
In Opera-land	Hillier
Growth	Dowson
Quatrains	Todhunter
The Dark Angel	Johnson
A Mood ('They have taken away my Lord, and I know not where they have laid Him')	Greene
A Mystical Prayer to the Masters of the Elements – Finvarra, Feacra, and Caolte	Yeats
Hesperides	Le Gallienne
Acknowledgment [*sic*]: to H. E. T.	Radford
Night: After All	Rolleston
Saint Anthony	Ellis

To O. E.	Rhys
A Variation Upon Love	Symons
A Secret of the Sea	Plarr
In an Old Library	Todhunter
The Garden of Shadow	Dowson
The Memorial Garden	Hillier
The Cap and Bells	Yeats
The Coming of War	Johnson
Lady Macbeth (For a Picture by John S. Sargent, A. R. A.)	Greene
Time's Monotone	Le Gallienne
The Shelley Memorial: The Master's Speech	Radford
The Wail of the Decadent	Radford
The Old Shepherd	Ellis
Midsummer Day	Hillier
'Ah, dans ces mornes séjours Les jamais sont les toujours.'	Dowson
On Great Sugarloaf	Greene
Celtic Speech	Johnson
The Night-Jar	Plarr
The Song of the Old Mother	Yeats
The First Spring Day	Todhunter
An Ode to Spring	Le Gallienne
A Presiding Examiner	Radford
A Rhyme on Rhyme	Ellis

Appendix III

A REVIEW OF NUMBER ONE OF THE *YELLOW BOOK* (The *Athenaeum*, 21 April, 1894):

THE first volume of the *Yellow Book* (Mathews and Lane), an illustrated quarterly, evidently aims at novelty, and yet it is not unlike in appearance the annual volumes of *Chatterbox* and other periodicals for young people. The opening article, Mr. Henry James's story, is the best piece of writing in the volume. Dr. Garnett and Mr. Saintsbury have also furnished excellent contributions. On the other hand, Mr. Le Gallienne's verses, which follow Mr. James's tale, are too artificial to be poetry, and Mr. Beerbohm's 'Defence of Cosmetics' is silly. Mr. Sickert's illustrations are not to our taste, and Mr. Beardsley's portrait of Mrs. Patrick Campbell is libellous. The *Yellow Book* will need to be better edited if it is to succeed.

Appendix IV

IN the August 1896 number of *The Savoy*, (pp. 91–93), appeared the following article by Arthur Symons, its editor:

A LITERARY CAUSERIE:

On a Book of Verses

A book of delicate, mournful, almost colourless, but very fragrant verses was lately published by a young poet whom I have the privilege to know somewhat intimately. Whether a book so essentially poetic, and at the same time so fragile in its hold on outward things, is likely to appeal very much to the general public, for which verse is still supposed to be written, it scarcely interests me to conjecture. It is a matter of more legitimate speculation, what sort of person would be called up before the mind's eye of any casual reader, as the author of love-poetry so reverent and so disembodied. A very ghostly lover, I suppose, wandering in a land of perpetual twilight, holding a whispered 'colloque sentimental' with the ghost of an old love:

> *'Dans le vieux parc solitaire et glacé*
> *Deux spectres ont évoqué le passé.'*

That is not how I have seen my friend, for the most part; and the contrast between the man as I have seen him and the writer of verses as I read them, is to me the most attractive interest of a book which I find singularly attractive. He will not mind, I know, if I speak of him with some of that frankness which we reserve usually for the dead, or with which we sometimes honour our enemies; for he is of a complete indifference to these things, as I shall assure myself over again before these lines are printed.

I do not remember the occasion of our first meeting, but I remember seeing him casually, at railway-stations, in a semi-literary tavern which once had a fantastic kind of existence, and sometimes, at night, in various part of the Temple, before I was more than slightly his acquaintance. I was struck then by a look and manner of pathetic charm, a sort of Keats-like face, the face of a demoralized Keats, and by something curious in the contrast of a manner exquisitely refined, with an appearance generally somewhat dilapidated. That impression was only accentuated, later on, when I came to know him, and the manner of his life, much more intimately. I think I may date my first real impression of what one calls 'the real man'—as if it were more real than the poet of the disembodied verses!—from an evening in which he first introduced me to those charming supper-houses, open all night through, the cabman's shelters. There were four of us, two in evening dress, and we were welcomed, cordially and without comment, at a little place near the Langham; and, I recollect, very hospitably entertained. He was known there, and I used to think he was always at his best in a cabmen's shelter. Without a certain sordidness in his surroundings, he was never quite comfortable, never quite himself; and at those places you are obliged to drink nothing stronger than coffee or tea. I liked to see him occasionally, for a change, drinking nothing stronger than coffee or tea. At Oxford, I believe, his favourite form of intoxication had been haschisch; afterwards he gave up this somewhat elaborate experiment in visionary sensation for readier means of oblivion; but he returned to it, I remember, for at least one afternoon, in a company of which I had been the gatherer, and of which I was the host. The experience was not a very successful one; it ended in what should have been its first symptom, immoderate laughter. It was disappointing, and my charming, expectant friends, disappointed.

Always, perhaps a little consciously, but at least always sincerely, in search of new sensations, my friend found what was for him the supreme sensation in a very passionate and tender adoration of the most escaping of all ideals, the ideal of youth. Cherished, as I imagine, first only in the abstract, this search after the immature, the ripening graces which time can but spoil in the ripening, found itself at the journey's end, as some of his friends thought, a little prematurely. I was never of their opinion. I only saw twice, and for a few moments only, the young girl to whom most of his verses were to be written, and whose presence in his life may be held to account for much of that astonishing contrast between the broad outlines of his life and work. The situation seemed to me of the most exquisite and appropriate impossibility. She had the gift of evoking, and, in its way, of retaining, all that was most delicate, sensitive, shy, typically poetic, in a nature which I can only compare to a weedy garden, its grass trodden down by many feet, but with one small, carefully-tended flower-bed, luminous with lilies. I used to think, sometimes, of Verlaine and his 'girl-wife', the one really profound passion, certainly, of that passionate career; the charming, child-like creature, to whom he looked back, at the end of his life, with an unchanged tenderness and disappointment: 'Vous n'avez rien compris à ma simplicité,' as he lamented. In the case of my friend there was, however, a sort of virginal devotion, as to a Madonna; and I think had things gone happily, to a conventionally happy ending, he would have felt (dare I say?) that his ideal had been spoilt.

But, for the good fortune of poets, things never do go happily with them, or to conventionally happy endings. So the wilder wanderings began, and a gradual slipping into deeper and steadier waters of oblivion. That curious love of the sordid, so common an affectation of the modern decadent, and with him so expressively genuine, grew upon him, and dragged him into yet more sorry corners of a life which was never exactly 'gay' to him. And now, indifferent to most things, in the shipwrecked quietude of a sort of self-exile, he is living, I believe, somewhere on a remote foreign sea-coast. People will complain, probably, in his verses, of what will seem to them the factitious melancholy, the factitious idealism, and (peeping through at a few rare moments) the factitious suggestions of riot. They will see only a literary affectation where in truth there is as poignant a note of personal sincerity as in the more explicit and arranged confessions of less admirable poets. Yes, in these few, evasive, immaterial snatches of song, I find, implied for the most part, hidden away like a secret, all the fever and turmoil and the unattained dreams of a life which has itself had much of the swift, disastrous, and suicidal energy of genius.

Bibliography of Works Cited

Banville, Theodore de. *Petit Traité de Poésie Française*. Paris, 1872.

Beckson, Karl. 'New Dates for the Rhymers' Club', ELT XIII, 1 (1970).

——. 'The Rhymers' Club,' *Yeats Studies*, I. Dublin, 1971.

Boyd, Ernest A. *Ireland's Literary Renaissance*. Dublin, 1916.

Brégy, Katherine. 'Ernest Dowson: An Interpretation,' *Catholic World*, November, 1914.

Burdett, Osbert. *The Beardsley Period*. London, 1925.

Croft-Cooke, Rupert. *Feasting with Panthers*. London, 1967.

Davidson, John. *John Davidson: A Selection of His Poems*. ed. M. Lindsay. London, 1961.

Dowson, Ernest, *Poems*, ed. A. Symons. London, 1905.

——. *The Letters of Ernest Dowson*, ed. D. Flower and H. Maas. London, 1967.

——. *The Poems of Ernest Dowson*, ed. M. Longaker. Philadelphia, 1962.

——. *The Poetical Works of Ernest Dowson*, ed. D. Flower. London, 1934.

——. *The Stories of Ernest Dowson*, ed. M. Longaker. London, 1946.

——. *Verses*. London, 1896.

Eliot, T. S. *The Sacred Wood*. University Paperbacks, London, 1960.

——. *Selected Essays*. London, 1932.

——. A Critical Note on Arthur Symons, *Criterion*, January, 1930, 357.

'Field, Michael' (Katherine Bradley and Edith Cooper). *Works and Days*. London, 1933.

Fletcher, Ian. 'Bedford Park: Aesthete's Elysium?' in *Romantic Mythologies*, ed. Ian Fletcher. London, 1967.

Gannon, Patricio. *Poets of the Rhymers' Club*. Buenos Aires, 1953.

Gawsworth, John. 'The Dowson Legend', *Essays by Divers Hands*, XVII (1938).

Gerber, Helmut E. 'The Nineties, Beginning, End or Transition?' *Edwardians & Late Victorians*, ed. R. Ellmann. New York, 1960.

Gilbert, W. S. and Sullivan, Sir Arthur. *Patience*. London, 1881.

Goldfarb, Russell M., 'The Dowson Legend Today', *SEL* IV (Autumn, 1964), 653–662.

Gray, John. *Silverpoints*. London, 1893.

Harris, Frank. *Contemporary Portraits*. London, 1915.

Harris, Wendell. 'Innocent Decadence: The Poetry of the *Savoy*', *PMLA*, LXXVII (1962), 629–636.

Hind, C. Lewis. *Napthali.* New York, 1926.
Hone, Joseph. *W. B. Yeats.* London, 1962.
Hough, Graham. *The Last Romantics.* London, 1947.
Jeffares, A. N. *W. B. Yeats, Man and Poet.* London, 1949.
Jepson, Edgar. *Memories of a Victorian.* London, 1933.
——. 'The Real Ernest Dowson', *Academy* (November, 1907).
Johnson, Lionel. *The Art of Thomas Hardy.* London, 1894.
——. *The Complete Poems of Lionel Johnson*, ed. I. Fletcher. London, 1953.
——. 'A Note Upon the Practice and Theory of Verse at the Present Time Obtaining in France', *Century Guild Hobby Horse* (April, 1891), 61.
——. *The Poetical Works of Lionel Johnson*, ed. Ezra Pound. London, 1915.
——. *Post Liminium: Essays and Critical Papers*, ed. Whittemore. London, 1911.
——. *Some Winchester Letters of Lionel Johnson*, ed. Anon., London, 1919.
Kipling, Rudyard. *Barrack-Room Ballads.* London, 1892.
Le Gallienne, Richard. *English Poems.* London, 1892.
——. *New Poems.* London, 1910.
——. *Retrospective Reviews: A Library Log.* London, 1896.
——. *The Romantic '90s.* London, 1925.
Lhombreaud, Roger. *Arthur Symons, A Critical Biography.* London, 1963.
Longaker, Mark. *Ernest Dowson.* Philadelphia, 1945.
MacNeice, Louis. *The Poetry of W. B. Yeats.* New York, 1941.
May, J. Lewis. *John Lane and the Nineties.* London, 1936.
Moore, George. *Ave.* London, 1911.
——. *Avowals.* London, 1924.
Munro, John M. 'A Previously Unpublished Letter from Ernest Dowson to Arthur Symons', *Études Anglaises*, XVII: 3 (1964), 285–287.
Nelson, James G. *The Early Nineties: A View From the Bodley Head.* Cambridge, Mass., 1971.
Odd Volume Year Boke, III. London, 1892.
Pater, Walter. *Marius the Epicurean.* New York, 1935.
——. *The Selected Works of Walter Pater*, ed. R. Aldington. London, 1948.
Plarr, Victor. *Ernest Dowson, 1888–1897: Reminiscences, Unpublished Letters, and Marginalia.* London, 1914.
Rhymers' Club, The Book of the. London, 1892.
——. Review article, Anon., *Church Quarterly*, XXXV (October, 1892), 201.
——. Review article, Anon., *Daily Chronicle*, 26 February, 1892.
——. Review article, Anon., *Daily News*, 20 February, 1892.
——. Review article, Anon., *Star*, 11 February, 1892.
——. Review article, Thomson, G. R., *Academy*, 26 March, 1892.
Rhymers' Club, The Second Book of the. London, 1894.
——. Review article, *Athenaeum*, 25 August, 1894.
Rhys, Ernest, *Everyman Remembers.* London, 1931.
——. *Letters from Limbo.* London, 1936.
——. *Wales England Wed.* London, 1940.
Richards, Grant. *Author Hunting.* New York, 1934.
——. *Memories of a Misspent Youth.* New York, 1933.
Roberts, Morley. 'The Rhymers' Club', *John O'London's Weekly*, 30 September, 1933.
Robinson, James K. 'A Neglected Phase of the Aesthetic Movement: English Parnassianism', *PMLA*, 68 II (1953), 733–754.
Rothenstein, William. *Men and Memories.* 2 vols. New York, 1931.
Santayana, George. *The Middle Span.* New York, 1945.
Savoy, The, ed. A. Symons. January, April, July—December, 1896.
Sherard, R. H. *Twenty Years in Paris.* London, 1905.
Stanford. Derek. *Three Poets of the Rhymers' Club*, Manchester, 1974.
Starkie, Enid. *From Gautier to Eliot.* London, 1960.

Symons, Arthur. *Amoris Victima*. London, 1896.
——. *The Café Royal and Other Essays*. London, 1923.
——. *Cities, Sea-coasts and Islands*. London, 1917.
——. *Days and Nights*. London, 1890.
——. 'The Decadent Movement in Literature', *Harper's Monthly Magazine*, XXXVII (November, 1893), 858–867.
——. *An Introduction to the Study of Browning*. London, 1886.
——. 'A Literary Causerie', *The Savoy*, August, 1896.
——. *London Nights*. London, 1895.
——. *Plays, Acting and Music*. London, 1903.
——. *Poems*. London, 1901; 1906 (2nd ed.); 1919, 2 vols. (3rd ed.).
——. *Silhouettes*. London, 1892.
——. *Studies in Prose and Verse*. London, 1904.
——. *Studies in Seven Arts*. London, 1906.
——. *A Study of Walter Pater*. London, 1932.
——. *The Symbolist Movement in Literature*. London, 1900. (Imprint date, 1899). I have used the Dutton 'Everyman' reprint, ed. Richard Ellmann (New York, 1958).
——. 'Paul Verlaine', *National Review*, June 1892.
——. 'Verlaine', *North American Review*, May 1915, 745–746.
Temple, Ruth Z. *The Critic's Alchemy*. New York, 1953.
Thomas, W. R. 'Ernest Dowson at Oxford', *Nineteenth Century*, April 1928.
Tillotson, Geoffrey. *Essays in Criticism and Research*. Cambridge, England, 1942.
Verlaine, Paul. *Dédicaces*. Paris, 1890.
Wade, Allan. *A Bibliography of the Writings of W. B. Yeats*. London, 1951.
Waugh, Arthur. *Memories*. London, 1924.
——. *Tradition and Change*. New York, 1919.
Weygandt, Cornelius. *The Time of Yeats*. New York, 1937.
——. *Tuesdays at Ten*. Philadelphia, 1928.
Wilde, Oscar. *The Picture of Dorian Gray*. London, 1891.
Yeats, W. B. *Autobiographies*. London, 1961.
——. *The Celtic Twilight*. London, 1893.
——. *The Collected Poems of W. B. Yeats*. London, 1950.
——. *The Countess Kathleen and Various Legends and Lyrics*. London, 1892.
——. *Essays and Introductions*. London, 1961.
——. ed., *Fairy and Folk Tales of the Irish Peasantry*, London, 1888.
——. *The Letters of W. B. Yeats*, ed. A. Wade. New York, 1955.
——. *Letters to the New Island*, ed. H. Reynolds. Cambridge, Mass., 1934.
——. 'Modern Poetry', *The Listener*, No. 405, 14 October, 1936.
——. ed., *The Oxford Book of Modern Verse*. Oxford, 1936.
——. 'The Rhymers' Club', *Boston Pilot*, 23 April, 1892.
——. *The Wanderings of Oisin and Other Poems*. London, 1889.
Yeats, W.B., and Johnson, Lionel. *Poetry and Ireland*. Dundrum, 1908.
Yellow Book, The. ed. H. Harland. 13 vols. 1894–1897.

Manuscripts

British Museum. Add. MS. 46363:

ALS Lionel Johnson to Campbell Dodgson.

ALS Carnegy Johnson to Campbell Dodgson.

British Museum. Ashley B658:

ALS Lionel Johnson to Edmund Gosse.

A. post-card, Ernest Dowson to Henry Davray.

Index